What people are saying about
Why Did God Give Us Emotions:

"Reneau Peurifoy has done it again. Another insightful book on the human dilemma, done in his usual artful, instructive, and clear manner . . . Reneau is a gifted communicator, and helps make the seemingly complicated issues understandable to his readers. *Why did God Give Us Emotions?* is a strong tool in helping us mere mortals understand how to integrate a knowledge of God into our emotions. The reading of this book will reap rich benefits."

REV. N. RHODES PRINGLE, Senior Pastor,
Antelope Road Christian Fellowship, Citrus Heights, CA.

"Finally! A Christian book that discusses, explores, and deals with emotions, such as depression, anxiety, and anger in a Biblical, scientific, and therapeutic way . . . I believe this book will show you how you can control and use your emotions in a way that glorifies God."

TONY DONATO, MS, MFT, LPC

"Unlike other books which offer very little practical advice, this book is full of wisdom and insight the reader can immediately apply. I am certain many will find freedom within its pages. From beginning to end, it calls readers to contemplate God's part in their emotions. I personally can't wait to recommend this book to clients. I think it will make a wonderful complement to their therapeutic process."

KRYSTA DANCY MA, MFTI

"Your book undertakes a comprehensive and practical treatment of the subject that does not stoop to self-help trendiness and nostrums but instead takes a high road. You offer insights both from medicine and psychology as well as from scriptural study. Anyone who is looking for a broad and well-founded understanding of emotions and how to deal with them will find what they are looking for in your book."

PAUL HAWLEY, Editorial Consultant

"A wonderful book that everyone should read! . . . As a Christian, registered nurse I realize how difficult it can be to understand our emotions at times. *Why Did God Give Us Emotions?* helped me to look more deeply into myself for clarification of some of my emotions. After reading this book I am able to better understand patients and their emotions during their time of stress in the hospital."

BARBARA P., RN

"Mr. Peurifoy has an astounding ability to get right to the heart of any matter, and his insights are profound. My husband and I have both read his books, did the recommended activities at the end of the chapters, and found our lives transformed. His latest book is a revelation, shining a light on the darkest corners of our emotions, and guiding us to a closer relationship with God."

RACHAEL D.

"The clarity of Mr. Peurifoy's writing challenged me to grow in areas that I did not even realize were there! I so much enjoyed this book that I will continue to reread it."

JACQUELYN NEAL

"I found this book to be relevant and insightful. The information and exercises have been very helpful in finding new understanding in why I feel the emotions I feel, and in being able to process these emotions in a manner that is healthier and more constructive than before."

ANNETTE S.

"Reneau Peurifoy has a special gift for explaining emotions and clarifying why we have them. This book in destined to become a great support to many people who have questions regarding their God-given emotions."

WARREN P.

Why did God give us
Emotions?

A BIBLICAL PERSPECTIVE ON WHAT SCIENCE HAS
DISCOVERED ABOUT EMOTIONS

BY RENEAU PEURIFOY, M.A.

LifeSkills Publications
Citrus Heights, California

Cover design by Lauri Worthington, Martino Creative
Interior design by Pat Reinheimer
Photo of Mr. Peurifoy by Jessica Giblin

Published by LifeSkills Publications
Citrus Heights, CA

Printed in the United States of America

Publisher's Cataloging-in-Publication

    Peurifoy, Reneau Z.
       Why did God give us emotions? / by Reneau Peurifoy.
       p. cm.
       Includes index.
       LCCN 2009906686
       ISBN-13: 978-0-929437-16-3
       ISBN-10: 0-929437-16-0

       1. Emotions--Religious aspects.   I. Title.

    BL65.E46P48 2009   204'.4
                           QBI09-600109

First Printing September 2009

10 9 8 7 6 5 4 3 2 1

CONTENTS

PREFACE

I did not grow up in a Christian home. However, my mother wanted my brother and me to have some moral training, so she would drop us off at a Baptist church where we attended Sunday school. She would then pick us up and take us home. While I do not ever remember formally accepting Christ as my savior during my childhood, I do remember that I considered Him a friend. I would often have long conversations with Him, especially when I was angry or hurt.

When I was eight, my father ended a twenty-one-year career with the navy and we moved to the outskirts of Sacramento, California. I enjoyed church and helping in Sunday school and continued to attend faithfully until I reached junior high school. My parents did not object to my going to church, but they also did not really encourage or support my attendance. So around the seventh grade, I stopped going. I still considered Jesus to be a good friend; however, my junior high school eyes saw a lot of hypocrisy in those attending church. Deciding that I could know God on my own, I quit attending church.

During high school I turned to science as my source of truth. I was even given the nickname "Spock" by some of my friends because I reminded them of Mr. Spock in the TV series *Star Trek* that was popular at the time. I graduated from high school in 1967, the year of the "summer of love" in the not-too-distant Haight-Ashbury district of San Francisco. While I was never a "hippie", the influence of the movement was certainly felt in Sacramento. This was especially true at the junior college I began attending. I spent the next two years drifting through college and playing blues guitar.

In 1969 I joined a Buddhist group and became an active member. During this time I advanced in their study department and became a teacher of their doctrine. This was when I met my wife, Michiyo. After five years I became disillusioned with Buddhism and turned to New Age teachings. After another five years, I became disillusioned with New Age teachings, and psychology became my new truth as I pursued my master's in counseling in preparation to become a marriage and family therapist. During this time my first child, a son, was born. When he turned four, I decided it was time for him to go to church, the way I had, so he could receive moral training.

At the time I was developing a home study mail-order program for people with panic disorder. I knew the lady who was helping design my material was a Christian so I asked about her church, and she invited me to attend. I began taking my son and attending the worship service while he was in Sunday school. I had not really read anything about the Christian faith in all my years since leaving the church and only remembered the stories and precepts I had been taught in Sunday school. Thus, as a young adult I considered the Christian faith to be somewhat simplistic. Now, I heard the gospel from an adult perspective, and it captured me. My search to find God was over, and I was baptized on December 2, 1984.

When I completed my first book, *Anxiety, Phobias & Panic: Taking Charge and Conquering Fear* in 1988, I knew that I wanted to write a companion version from a Christian perspective. However, after being back in church for only four years and with so many conflicting ideas from my wanderings still in my head, I knew I wasn't ready. So, I had the wife of our head pastor write a supplement to the first book. Although it was not what I envisioned, it was a start.

In 1995 I started attending classes through Fuller Seminary's extension program to deepen my understanding of the Bible. At this time I learned Greek and began studying the New Testament in Greek. A year later I wrote the first draft of this book but realized after several chapters that I was not yet mature enough in faith or understanding to write the book I wanted to write. So I put it aside. I made another attempt to write it about five years later, but again was dissatisfied with the results.

Now, after twenty years of being humbled and growing in Christ, I believe that God has helped me write a book that will be useful to many. From the very start I've had two goals: I wanted to look at what science has learned about emotions from a biblical perspective, and I wanted to do it in a way that would strengthen the readers' walk with God. Over the last two decades I've seen the strengths of science and psychology in helping people and making our lives more comfortable. I've also become acutely aware of the inability of science and psychology to address the true source of human misery: sin and our separation from God.

My prayer is that you are blessed by what I've written.

Reneau, 2009

CHAPTER 1

THE MYSTERY OF EMOTIONS

Jerry and Kathy had been married for only a year when they heard the news that Kathy was pregnant. The doctor's report of Kathy's pregnancy brought them both a joy they had never before experienced. A short time later, their joy was multiplied when they learned that Kathy would be giving birth to twins. They constantly thanked God as they decorated the nursery that would soon shelter their new arrivals. Then, on the day that Jerry and Kathy went to the hospital for the delivery, tragedy struck. The first baby, a girl, struggled to live but died after only an hour. The second twin girl was delivered still born. As Kathy wept, Jerry sat too stunned to respond to the stabbing pain that had suddenly overtaken him.

In an instant, joy had been transformed into a grief that was almost too much to bear. In the days that followed, Jerry and Kathy wondered if their faith had failed them. If it hadn't, why were they so angry over their tragic loss? As they struggled with the flood of emotions, it seemed like it was all too much, too sudden, too confusing.

Emotions are a mysterious gift. As with Kathy and Jerry, they take us to heights of ecstasy then dash us on the rocks of despair. But emotions do much more than this. They can bind us together and tear us apart. They can move some to noble acts of courage and self-sacrifice while in others they are the force behind terrible acts of evil and destruction.

Why did God make us this way? How are we supposed to manage this wonderful and mystifying gift we call emotions? In the pages that follow, you will explore these two simple, yet profound questions. In the process of seeking answers, you will gain skills that can help you manage your emotions more effectively, and learn how your emotions can help you both understand God more fully and draw closer to Him.

THE ELEPHANT NATURE OF EMOTIONS

A well-known Indian parable tells of six blind men who encounter an elephant for the first time. As each one touches a different part of the elephant, they arrive at conflicting conclusions as to what the elephant is like. The first man touches the elephant's leg and states that it is like a pillar. The second touches the tail and declares it to be like a rope. The third touches the trunk and says it is like the thick branch of a tree. The fourth touches the ear and shouts that it is like a big fan. The fifth touches the side of the elephant and declares it to be like a huge wall. The sixth touches the tusk and says it is like a spear. Although each man's perception of the part he touched is accurate, none has really understood the true nature of the elephant.

The same type of misunderstanding can happen when

individual aspects of emotions are studied without stepping back periodically to see how they interconnect. The four main aspects of emotions most often studied separately include:

- *The subjective nature of emotions:* This includes how they make you feel, how they focus your energy and attention, and how they urge you to take actions to obtain the things you want and avoid the things you don't want. This aspect of emotions also includes the experiential understanding of events and concepts that is much more powerful than simple knowledge.
- *The physical side of emotions:* This includes the various parts of the brain associated with emotions, the physical reactions they cause in your body, and the ways injury, illness, or other malfunctions of the brain can affect how you think and feel.
- *The mental side of emotions:* This includes the role that your thoughts and beliefs play in generating emotions and how emotions, in turn, affect your thoughts.
- *The spiritual side of emotions:* This includes the way emotions reveal both your true character and the nature of your relationship with God as you struggle to live in a broken world. It also includes the way emotions give us insights about the nature of God.

In the next seven chapters you will begin your exploration of emotions. Like the blind men, you will look at each of these four basic aspects of emotions separately. Once you have explored each aspect individually, you will be ready to step back in chapter 10 and see them as parts of a whole and how each part interacts with the others. However, before beginning our journey, I would like to address two issues briefly.

ARE SOME EMOTIONS GOOD AND OTHERS BAD?

Christians sometimes spend a great deal of time pondering whether some emotions, such as love, are good and others, such as anger, are bad. It is similar to wondering whether your hands are good or bad. Emotions, like every other aspect of your being, were originally intended to help you enjoy and serve God. However, just as the actions of your hands can be pleasing or abhorrent to God, your emotions can also serve good or evil. What we need to focus on is the source of the emotion or action.

When the Pharisees saw that Jesus' disciples were not performing a ritual washing before eating, they questioned Him about it. After pointing out how the Pharisees had become consumed with ritual and failed to do what God commanded, Jesus called the crowd to him and said, "Listen and understand. What goes into a man's mouth does not make him 'unclean,' but what comes out of his mouth, that is what makes him 'unclean'" (Matthew 15:10–11). When Peter questioned him further on this point Jesus explained that "the things that come out of the mouth come from the heart, and these make a man 'unclean.' For out of the heart come evil thoughts, murder, adultery, sexual immorality, theft, false testimony, slander. These are what make a man 'unclean'" (18-20). Keep in mind that when the New Testament refers to the heart, it is not just looking at it as the center of emotions as modern English does. Instead, the New Testament uses the heart to represent your entire inner being: your mind, desires, emotions, spirit, and soul.

The point is that the source of evil lies in a mind and heart tainted with sin. The actions you take and the emotions you experience are just the outer expression of what is in your heart and mind. Yielding to the Holy Spirit transforms your inner being into what God intended it to be. As this occurs, your emotions, desires, and thoughts are transformed so they function more closely to what God intends.

DON'T JUST READ, EXPERIENCE

Many different types of people will be reading this book. Some will simply be reading it out of intellectual curiosity. Others will be reading it because they or a loved one is struggling with some emotional issue in their life. Regardless of the reason, I encourage you to take your time as you read through the book and do the Recommended Activities at the end of each chapter before you go on to the next. While simply reading the information will provide you with new insights, many of the ideas discussed in the following chapters cannot be fully grasped until you experience them through the activities at the end of each chapter.

As you work through the activities for a given chapter, you will probably find that some are easy, while others are more difficult for you or make you uncomfortable. The easy activities probably address aspects of emotions with which you are comfortable, healthy areas of your life, or skills that you have mastered. The difficult or uncomfortable activities probably involve areas of your life where growth or healing is needed or call on skills that you have not yet developed. Because of this, you may be inclined to spend less time with some activities and more with others. That's fine, as long as you spend some time doing all the exercises. Even though a particular exercise may seem uncomfortable or irrelevant to you at first, the results of doing it may surprise you.

If you are reading this book because you have issues that you've struggled with for a long time, keep in mind that you have spent your entire life developing your current emotional, thinking, and behavior patterns. Changing any one of them takes time. More importantly, changing them into what God wants them to be depends on your relationship with God and the degree to which you allow the Holy Spirit to control your daily walk. Be patient and trust that the Holy Spirit is involved with the process and moving you along at a pace that is just right for you. In fact, when an important change occurs, you probably won't even notice it until later. This is how growth takes place. If you have a strong commitment to use this book as it is designed to be used — to do the reading and apply as many of the suggestions as possible even when they seem frivolous or beside the point — not only will you gain a fuller understanding of why God gave you emotions and the role they play in your life, but you will also gain new skills in managing your emotions in a way that pleases God.

In closing this chapter, I join with Paul and pray that God will use this book in such a way that it will help you

> always honor and please the Lord, and your [life] will produce every kind of good fruit. All the while, you will grow as you learn to know God better and better.
>
> [I] also pray that you will be strengthened with all his glorious power so you will have all the endurance and patience you need. May you be filled with joy, always thanking the Father. He has enabled you to share in the inheritance that belongs to his people, who live in the light. For he has rescued us from the kingdom of darkness and transferred us into the Kingdom of his dear Son, who purchased our freedom and forgave our sins. (Colossians 1:10–14, NLT)

▶RECOMMENDED ACTIVITIES

ASK GOD TO USE THIS BOOK TO HELP YOU DRAW CLOSER TO HIM

It is no accident that you discovered this book and decided to read it. There is something in it that God wants you to learn. The best way to ensure that you don't miss what God wants to reveal to you is to invite Him to participate in your reading. Each time you pick up this book or work in your journal, take a moment to ask God to open your heart and mind to the things He wants to reveal to you through this book.

KEEP A JOURNAL AS YOU WORK THROUGH THE CHAPTERS

I strongly recommend that you keep a journal while you work through this book. A journal gives you a place to do the written exercises so you can refer back to them. It's also a natural place to make notes about what you are learning.

You don't need to use an expensive or fancy volume for your journal. A simple spiral-bound notebook is fine. Some like to record their thoughts on a computer. Feel free to choose whatever is most comfortable for you. As you work with your journal, keep in mind that privacy is essential, in order for you to write frankly and freely. Do not write for an "unseen audience" because attempting to please invisible watchers can cause you to lose much of the benefit of keeping a journal. You also do not need to write something every day. Although some do find that keeping a daily journal is best, others find that working in their journal two or three times a week best suits their situation.

As you add to your journal, keep in mind that its main value is not the permanent record it represents but the work you put into creating it. The act of writing is a powerful way to learn because it involves several parts of the brain. This is why written homework is a fundamental part of formal education. When you are grappling with emotional issues, a journal also helps you be more objective. People often find that thinking about their emotions on a piece of paper is much easier than thinking about them in their head.

TAKE A FEW MINUTES TO DECIDE WHAT YOU WANT TO GET OUT OF THIS BOOK

Take some time now to answer the following two questions:

- Why am I reading this book?
- What do I want to get out of it?

Record your answers in your journal. Here are examples of what four different people wrote:

I would like to understand my emotions more. Sometimes I get angry more than I should, and I would like to learn how to stop doing this.

I'm curious about how my emotions fit into God's plan for me.

I don't understand why my husband reacts like he does. I'd like to understand him better and learn how to not be so angry or hurt by some of the things he does.

I would like to understand why, being a Christian, I sometimes get very depressed . I have even considered suicide. I know this is wrong, but I can't seem to snap out of it.

CHAPTER 2

THE SUBJECTIVE SIDE OF EMOTIONS

I n the first chapter you learned that emotions can be studied from four distinct viewpoints: subjective, physical, mental, and spiritual. In this chapter we begin exploring the first of these, the subjective side of emotions. Let's begin by considering John who had just finished completing the coursework and required hours of driver's training needed to receive a driver's license.

Soon after he had received his license, his parents, proud of their son's accomplishment, asked him to go on an errand by himself that required him to travel a short distance on the local expressway. As he headed out, he put on his favorite music, cranked up the volume and was very pleased with his new freedom. As he began to move onto the expressway, he was singing with the music and thinking about how envious his friends at school would be.

Suddenly, he saw a car that he hadn't noticed coming into his lane. Without thinking, he slammed on the brakes and began swerving violently. Fortunately, there were no other vehicles close to him. This allowed him to regain control of the car and get to his destination safely even though he was somewhat shaken by the experience.

During his driver's training John had paid careful attention when his instructor told him of the need to constantly check his surroundings when merging onto an expressway. He had also understood the correct way to apply his brakes in a situation like this. However, like so many other things that he had learned, it was just information. John's experience now gave this information a new and deeper meaning and provided motivation for him to become a better driver. Indeed, afterwards he was more aware of his surroundings when getting on and off the expressway and more careful in how he applied his brakes.

This simple story illustrates two key roles of the subjective side of emotions: they give meaning to life's experiences, and they provide the motivation that drives our behavior.

Your Inner and Outer Worlds

The subjective side of emotions is part of what is often called your *subjective reality*. Your subjective reality includes everything you experience inside that no one else can experience directly. In contrast, objective reality includes everything you experience "outside of your skin" — everything that both you and others can see, touch, taste, hear, or smell and agree on. For example, both you and another can see, touch, smell, and taste a piece of cake. You and the other person might agree on the color of the cake and whether it tastes like lemon or chocolate. You might also agree that the cake is sweet.

Although you and the other person will share a common objective experience of the cake, your subjective experience could be quite different. You might find the taste and smell of the cake enjoyable while the other person may not like either one. The taste or smell might also trigger the memory of a joyful celebration you attended or a painful childhood experience, thoughts that the other person would not share. If you did describe your thoughts and enjoyment, they would not mean exactly the same thing to this person as they do to you. Even if you both agreed that you enjoyed the cake, neither of you would really know whether you were both enjoying the cake as much or in the same way. You would know only that you both had an enjoyable experience.

The same thing can be said for all our experiences. Because we have no way to "get inside" another person's head, we never really know exactly how another person is feeling or experiencing some event.

EMOTIONS AND MOTIVATION

The subjective side of emotions plays a key role in motivating you to take action. Indeed, as emotions become more intense, they produce a stronger urge to take action. This role of emotions can be seen in the original root of the word *emotion* which means "to move." You can still see this in the modern English word *e-motion*. Emotions tend to fall into one of three general groups: emotions like excitement or joy that are a response to needs being met, emotions like fear and anger that are a response to a threat, and emotions such as disappointment or sadness that are a response to a loss of some type.

For most people, the sudden and unexpected sound of breaking glass has been associated with danger and produces a strong emotional reaction. Because of this, if you are sitting at home reading or watching television and hear the sound of breaking glass, all your attention immediately shifts from what you are doing to the threatening sound. Your emotions then produce a strong urge to get up and find out what is going on.

This is what happened with John's near miss on the expressway. Prior to the near miss, he had little motivation to apply the information he had learned. Afterward, that information had been given an emotional stamp that motivated him to change his future behavior (This is discussed in detail in the next chapter).

EMOTIONS, EXPERIENCE, AND UNDERSTANDING

To understand fully the important role of the subjective side of emotions, we need to discuss how we have been created as "experiential" beings. The subjective, experiential aspect of life makes the difference between knowing something and understanding it. A person who cannot swim might read all sorts of information about swimming. This person would now have a thorough knowledge of swimming. However, true understanding would come only through the process of learning to swim and experiencing it directly.

This is true for two reasons. First, we have been created with physical bodies. Because we have physical bodies and live in a physical world, we need to experience things physically to understand them. You can see this in the way that a toddler learns about space. The toddler learns about distance and height through the experience of crawling and climbing.

Second, experience is necessary because it allows our emotions to sort the important from the unimportant. Experiences that affect you in some important way receive an emotional "stamp". The emotions associated with what you've learned then helps order and regulate your behavior by drawing your attention and energy away from less important information and activities towards more important ones.

Returning to the illustration of swimming, you can read about buoyancy and how water will support you and allow you to float on the water if you relax and don't struggle. However, the reality of being in water and learning to relax and trust that this information is true gives a physical meaning to what you've read that differs from simple knowledge. Both the fear that strikes when you tense and sink and the pleasure experienced when you relax prioritize the information and the actions associated with floating in water. These emotions then motivate the proper actions needed to float in the future.

The way experience and emotions interact to create understanding can also be clearly seen in the history of humankind. When the first two people, Adam and Eve, were created, God made it clear that they were created for His pleasure and fellowship. God established a hospitable, warm, intimate environment in which He and they could experience one another. After the fall, people lost their intimate relationship with God due to sin. As God's plan for the restoration of that relationship unfolded, He took individuals and generations through many different experiences that allowed them to begin to understand who He is and what His will is. A good example is His giving of the law, the Ten Commandments, to the Israelites.

God's people struggled for centuries to try to understand these rules for life and created all sorts of additional rules and traditions to ensure they were followed. However, the experience of the Israelites through a hundred generations, as recorded in the Old Testament, demonstrated clearly that knowledge of these rules, by itself, could not bring about the life and restoration God was planning. It was only when God lived and walked among us in flesh that we began to really understand them. Even more important, it is only through a dynamic and vital relationship with Christ that we experience God's love and care in a way that gives us the ability to truly understand the nature of God and what He wants for us.

This, then, brings us back to the tragic experience of Jerry and Kathy described at the beginning of the first chapter. Prior to experiencing the deaths of the twins, Jerry and Kathy would have been considered knowledgeable and committed Christians. However, as they looked back, it was clear to them they had expected to be sheltered from the evils of this world if they simply obeyed God and followed His will as best they could.

As time passed and they struggled with their grief, Jerry and Kathy experienced God working in their lives. This gave them a much deeper understanding of the brokenness of this world and the influence of sin on it. They experienced not only how God carries us through the tragedies that are such a common part of living in this evil age, but also how He can use those tragedies, if we yield to His leading, to transform us more and more into the image of Christ. New and deeper meaning came from passages such as these:

> I have told you these things, so that in me you may have peace. In this world you will have trouble. But take heart! I have overcome the world. (John 16:33)

> No temptation has seized you except what is common to man. And God is faithful; he will not let you be tempted beyond what you can bear. But when you are tempted, he will also provide a way out so that you can stand up under it. (1 Corinthians 10:13)

When tempted, no one should say, "God is tempting me." For God cannot be tempted by evil, nor does he tempt anyone. (James 1:13)

The stories describing the suffering and pain experienced by Joseph and Job in the Old Testament also took on new meaning along with passages that tell of the current state of the world such as, "the whole world is under the control of the evil one" (1 John 5:19). As time passed, Jerry and Kathy also saw how God cared for them by sending members of their church who became angels in human form as well as comfort through songs and messages that spoke to their pain and suffering.

Twenty years later, after experiencing how God carried them through their loss, things are quite different in the lives of Jerry and Kathy. They now have a healthy family of four children, three girls and a son, who have brought immeasurable joy. They learned through their devastating personal experience that their faith had not failed them and that God had not abandoned them. Both have reached a new level of maturity and confidence in the faithfulness of God.

Moreover, God has used this experience to equip them for a ministry that blesses others who are struggling with similar losses. Within two years of their own tragedy, they were called to sit with another young family who had lost a baby at birth. Their experience allowed them to comfort and care for this family in a way that simple knowledge could never have accomplished. By putting their trust in God at a moment of little understanding, God was able to use this experience to shape them into extensions of His heart and hands.

▶Recommended Activities

Keep a Record of Strong Emotions You Experience

Take a few minutes each day to record in your journal times when you experienced strong emotions, either positive or negative. Do not try to analyze why you reacted as you did. Simply record the following:

- What was taking place just before you experienced the strong emotion? Was the emotion related to what was happening at that time or did it seem to come from "out of the blue"?
- What did you feel? Be sure to use words that describe emotions such as *happy, sad, angry, excited, anxious*, or *depressed*. Avoid words that describe your situation such as *helpless, inadequate*, or *frustrated* as well as words that describe your mental state such as *confused* or *puzzled*.
- What thoughts did it trigger?
- What did you do as a result of experiencing this emotion?

Here are examples of what two different people wrote:

I was talking with several co-workers when one began talking about a trip he had taken to see his parents. I became very sad for no apparent reason and thought, "This is stupid. Why am I reacting this way?" I made a joke that changed the subject.

Several of my relatives came to visit, and I was playing a board game with them. I started to lose and began to feel very anxious and angry. I hid my feelings but was surprised at how intense they were.

BE AN ACTIVE MEMBER OF A SPIRIT-FILLED CHURCH

People often say that they don't need to be a member of a church to be a Christian or have a good relationship with God. This is one of Satan's more clever lies and keeps many Christians stagnant in their faith and spiritually weak. However, the Bible clearly teaches that the only way you can have life, grow, and bear fruit is to be connected to Christ. One of the most striking descriptions is in John:

> I am the true vine, and my Father is the gardener. He cuts off every branch in me that bears no fruit, while every branch that does bear fruit he prunes so that it will be even more fruitful. You are already clean because of the word I have spoken to you. Remain in me, and I will remain in you. No branch can bear fruit by itself; it must remain in the vine. Neither can you bear fruit unless you remain in me. (John 15:1–4)

The Bible also makes clear in a number of places that the church is the body of Christ and, as such, the place where we receive nourishment and care from Him. Paul is especially fond of this analogy as in the following passages:

> Christ is the head of the church, his body, of which he is the Savior. (Ephesians 5:23)

> No one ever hated his own body, but he feeds and cares for it, just as Christ does the church. (Ephesians 5:29)

> Just as each of us has one body with many members, and these members do not all have the same function, so in Christ we who are many form one body, and each member belongs to all the others. (Romans 12:4–5)

This is why the author of Hebrews urges his readers, "Let us not give up meeting together, as some are in the habit of doing, but let us encourage one another—and all the more as you see the Day approaching" (Hebrews 10:25). So while it is true that churches often fall far short of what God intended them to be, they are still the institution that He ordained as the place where we can learn about Him, learn how to love one another, grow spiritually, and spread the gospel. As a result, you will only develop a truly dynamic relationship with God and grow spiritually when you are a member of a healthy church.

While this can be difficult for people who have been disappointed or wounded by the church, it is still a necessary part of being a Christian. If you have had a bad experience in a church, keep in mind that not all churches are the same. Finding the right church will help heal the wounds you have suffered and reconnect you with the source of life.

One of the things to look for in a church is the presence of the Holy Spirit. Several things indicate that the Holy Spirit is active in a church. You will see evidence of the fruit of the Holy Spirit in the lives of the members: love, joy, peace, patience, kindness, goodness, faithfulness, gentleness, and self-control (Galatians 5:22–23). You will also see people coming to know Christ and lives being transformed.

If you are already both a member of a Spirit-filled church and an active participant in some sort of small group activity, continue with what you are doing! If not, you need to take three important steps to experience the importance of being connected to the body of Christ:

- Become part of a Spirit-filled church.
- Attend worship services regularly.

- Find activities outside of worship in which to participate that enable you to connect with fellow believers in a more intimate way.

If you are a member of a church but don't attend regularly, resolve to begin doing so. Be sure to ask God to give you both the motivation and the strength to carry out your resolution. Keep in mind the third point listed above: your attendance needs to go beyond simply showing up for the worship service. While this is an important first step, you also need to find some type of small group activity in which you can participate. This is where you form relationships and set the stage for God to reveal to you many deeper things about yourself and about life.

If you are wondering whether or not you are really connected to a church, ask yourself the following questions:

- Are there at least two people at the church who:
  - know you by first name?
  - talk to you regularly?
  - know about your life and its current problems and successes?
  - would miss you if you did not come?
  - would respond if you asked for help such as to be picked up from a doctor's appointment?
- Do you participate in a church activity other than the worship service at least twice a month?
- Does your church feel like a home to you?

If you did not answer yes to all these questions, look for a small group where you can begin to form relationships that go beyond mere surface familiarity.

If you are not a member of a church, several suggestions on

how find a church that's right for you can be found in Appendix 1: Suggestions on How to Find a Good Church. Be sure to read it before you begin your search and again when you are deciding on which church is best for you.

CHAPTER 3

THE PHYSICAL SIDE
OF EMOTIONS

Joe had experienced a deep sense of sadness and loneliness for many years. While he was growing up, there had been many problems in his family. As an adult, he had experienced a string of broken relationships and often found it difficult to get along with others. Joe thought his persistent sadness was simply due to his unhappy childhood and poor adult relationships. Yet there were periods when Joe was happy and outgoing. During these times, he plunged almost feverishly into work or church projects. Unfortunately, the good times never lasted long, and his sadness would soon return.

Joe had reached out to his church family on many occasions for prayer and had gone to several pastors and Christian counselors for help. However, his depression and sense of hopelessness recurred and persisted. Some of those closest to him had questioned his faith. Others told him that he was just not trying hard enough. If only he would pray more, read the Bible more, or work more diligently at applying the lessons taught in Sunday school, he would be a joyful Christian. One person even thought that Joe might be a closet alcoholic; another suggested that he was just playing some emotional game to get attention or sympathy from others.

Finally, Joe saw a pastor who urged him to see a psychiatrist he knew well and trusted. After a thorough evaluation, Joe was diagnosed with bi-polar disorder. Once he was put on the proper medications, he escaped the lingering depression and began to live a relatively normal life. His spiritual life blossomed, and, for the first time in his life, he felt like he was connecting with others in a deep and meaningful way.

Like many, Joe didn't know that emotional problems can have physical causes. Instead, he wrongly believed that his depression somehow was due to spiritual weakness or something he had done wrong even though he could not identify what that might be. While many emotional problems are primarily spiritual or psychological in nature, there are a wide variety of physical illnesses that can cause emotional problems. Sometimes a problem with the brain itself is the primary cause of an emotional problem.

THE BRAIN AS A SYMPHONY OF ACTIVITY

The Psalms declare, "I praise you because I am fearfully and wonderfully made; your works are wonderful" (Psalm 139:14). Even cynical Eliphaz, when talking to Job, says of God, "He performs wonders that cannot be fathomed, miracles that cannot be counted" (Job 5:9). Of all of God's creation, this is perhaps most true of the physical brain that God gave you. It weighs only three pounds, but it is estimated to contain about 100 billion cells.

What is even more incredible is the unimaginable number of connections that these cells make. The complexity of the activity in your brain dwarfs the volume of messages that pass among all of the phones in the world over the span of a day. What an awesome God we have who works on such a grand scale even inside our own bodies!

The human brain is so amazing and complex that, although we know a lot about how the brain works, there is a tremendous amount yet to be explained. In many ways we have just scratched the surface of understanding how emotions and the brain work. With that said, let's look at some of what we do know about the physical side of emotions.

The brain is often compared to a computer. It is described as having software, hardware, programs, and other computer-like components. Self-help books often use computer terms such as "reprogramming" to describe the process of changing beliefs and behaviors. However, both the make-up of the brain and the way it works set it apart from computers.

The cells that make up the brain, called neurons, differ completely from the transistors and other electronic components used in computers. One key difference is that electrical components communicate directly through electric signals. This limits computers to using a digital language based on ones and zeros. Communication between neurons (with a few exceptions in mammals) is a chemical process. Because neurons can use chemical messages to interact in any of several ways, neural communication is far more complex than what is found in computers. While the details of how the brain processes information are still largely a mystery, we do know that it is very different from the way that computer programs composed of linear, step-by-step instructions process information.

A better analogy for understanding the brain is to compare

it to an orchestra. In a large orchestra, there are several different sections: percussion, strings, woodwinds, and brass. Each section has its own part to play and must work smoothly with the other sections in order for a piece of music to sound right. If the strings come in at the wrong time or do not play their part correctly, the music as a whole suffers.

In a similar way, the brain has many different parts. Each part has its own job and must not only do that job correctly, but also coordinate with the other parts for us to experience life fully. Vision, for example, involves over forty areas of the brain. Some areas determine shapes, movement, and color, while other areas assign meaning to either the individual elements of what one is seeing or the overall pattern.

The amazing thing about this process is that it goes on primarily at an unconscious level making vision seem like a very simple activity. We glimpse the complexity of these unconscious processes only when people experience unusual types of head injuries. One example of this is known as "blind sight."

Blind sight is a rare condition in which a person who has experienced brain damage loses sight in one or both eyes but still has some elements of vision. Graham Young is one such person. A head injury in an automobile accident blinded his right eye so he can no longer see anything to his right. Curiously, however, even though he can no longer consciously perceive anything to that side, his right eye can still detect movement. When you move an object in the visual field of his right eye, he can tell you that there is movement up and down, sideways, and so on. However, he has no idea what he is "seeing". The explanation for this strange phenomenon is that while the main pathway to the visual centers has been damaged, a secondary pathway leading to the area of the brain that detects movement is still intact. This is what allows him to sense movement even though he does not know what is moving.

Cases such as Graham Young's demonstrate that the brain does a lot of information processing that we are totally unaware of. One of the clearest examples of this in everyday life is driving a car. Your brain is able to process the sights and sounds of the highway so that you are able to avoid obstacles and negotiate traffic while your conscious mind thinks about totally unrelated matters. While cruising down a highway, you often drive on "autopilot". You only become fully conscious of driving when something triggers emotions that cause you to shift your attention to what triggered those emotions. It might be a routine landmark that tells you when your turn is coming up, or it might be a sudden threat such as car swerving into your lane.

THE EMOTIONAL PART OF THE BRAIN

The part of the brain usually associated with emotions is called the limbic system. The limbic system is composed of several parts; we will look at two of them, the hippocampus and the amygdala. For now, each serves as a good example of the connection between the physical brain, your memories, and your emotions.

The *hippocampus* is a small curved structure. You have two, one on either side of the brain. These two structures have been identified as the part of the brain that creates memories. People whose hippocampi have been destroyed due to illness or injury are unable to create new memories. At the same time, since memories formed prior to the loss of the hippocampi remain, it is clear that they are not the place where memories are stored. Instead, the role of the hippocampi is to connect the various elements of the memory together for later recall. Unfortunately, just how this is done is still largely unknown.

The *amygdala* is an almond-shaped structure. As with the hippocampus, you have two, one at the lower end of each hippocampus. Research has shown that when animals or people experience a threat, the amygdalae spring into action and strengthen the memory, giving it a sort of "emotional stamp". For example, if you are in a car accident, the sights, sounds, and thoughts associated with the accident become signs of danger. When you experience any of these sensations in the future, they cause you to become anxious and more alert. In fact, research has shown that fearful responses can occur without the participation of any higher reasoning process. This is one of God's ways of protecting us, since we need to be aware of potential threats.

One curious aspect of the amygdalae and other areas of the brain that manage fear is that they are designed to *overreact* to possible signs of danger. For example, a person living where there are poisonous snakes will quickly learn to associate snakes with danger. The amygdalae will then immediately trigger the fight or flight response (see the next section) whenever the person perceives anything that might be a snake. After all, if you are walking in the woods, it is better to mistake a stick for a snake than a snake for a stick.

Keep in mind that this all occurs at an unconscious level. These parts of the brain allow you to react very quickly to danger without having to think about what is occurring. Unfortunately, events and objects that pose no threat can become associated with danger and trigger a fear response when you encounter them. This unconscious interpretation of harmless or even beneficial everyday situations as dangerous can interfere with your life in many ways. It is especially important in the development of anxiety-related problems.

For example Ramona experienced severe panic attacks for many years. When the attacks came, her heart would pound, she felt like she couldn't breathe, and she would sweat and sometimes even find her hands trembling. These attacks had caused her to limit her life and avoid many normal activities such as driving, going to a shopping mall, attending church, or being around lots of people. All these activities and places had become associated with danger because of the panic attacks she experienced. Thus, whenever she thought of them or tried to lead a normal life, her amygdalae would fire the danger circuits in her brain, and she would experience severe anxiety.

Like Joe, Ramona had sought counsel from godly men and women. Unfortunately, because they had little knowledge of her condition, their counsel was not effective and she received little relief from her symptoms. She was told that being healed was simply a matter of having enough faith. When she did not improve she was told that she was actively sabotaging other people's efforts to help her.

Eventually, Ramona did find someone who understood and properly diagnosed her condition as panic disorder. She was then able to address the physical as well as the mental and spiritual sides of this debilitating condition. To understand the physical side of this type of problem, we need to take a look at what is commonly called the fight or flight response.

THE FIGHT OR FLIGHT RESPONSE

Emotions are intimately connected with your body through your nervous system. This system has two basic parts, the *central nervous system*, composed of the brain and spinal cord, and the *peripheral nervous system* which includes all of the nerves leading away from and returning back to the central nervous system. The peripheral nervous system is also divided into two parts: the *voluntary* nervous system and the *autonomic* nervous system.

The voluntary nervous system, also called the somatic nervous system, is composed of the nerves that connect both to the voluntary muscles that move the various parts of the body (*motor* nerves) and those that transmit sensory information (*sensory* nerves). This system sends information from your eyes, ears, and other senses to the brain which then controls the actions that require thought, such as speaking, grasping an object, or walking by sending messages to your various muscles.

The autonomic nervous system is composed of all the nerves that connect to your internal organs, glands, and involuntary muscles. This system controls all the automatic activities that occur in your body like sweating, digestion, and breathing. The autonomic nervous system has two basic parts, the *sympathetic* and *parasympathetic* divisions. The sympathetic division is responsible for what is commonly referred to as the fight or flight response. This response is designed to activate the body quickly and prepare it to either fight or flee from danger. When the danger has passed, the parasympathetic division quiets the body and returns it to normal functioning. All these parts of the nervous system can be diagrammed as follows:

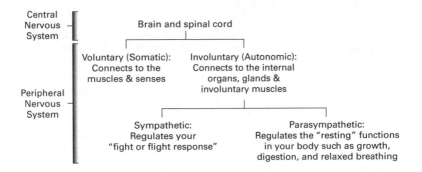

Central Nervous System — Brain and spinal cord

Peripheral Nervous System —

Voluntary (Somatic): Connects to the muscles & senses

Involuntary (Autonomic): Connects to the internal organs, glands & involuntary muscles

Sympathetic: Regulates your "fight or flight response"

Parasympathetic: Regulates the "resting" functions in your body such as growth, digestion, and relaxed breathing

The part of the above system that interests us is the fight or flight response. When the fight or flight response is triggered, it releases increased amounts of adrenaline (epinephrine) and related chemicals into the bloodstream. This response provides the added strength and stamina and the quickened reactions that help soldiers survive in battle, athletes perform their best, and people facing dangerous situations respond more effectively.

Fortunately, in our modern technological world, we face fewer physical dangers requiring strenuous action than did our ancestors or those living in less industrialized areas of the world. Most of the threats we face today are not life-threatening. Instead, they involve issues such as the loss of love, status, prestige, or our sense of belonging and significance. Usually, these losses do not require an immediate physical response.

Unfortunately, our bodies respond to any threat as if it does require an immediate physical response. So, when you are embarrassed and feel threatened by what others think, your body triggers the fight or flight response and begins gearing up to physically run away or to fight even though such action is not required.

Some individuals, like Ramona from the previous section, experience exaggerated fight or flight symptoms that seem to occur for no apparent reason or in response to situations that pose no real threat. In Ramona's case, everyday activities had become associated with fear. Whenever she thought about or encountered them, her amygdalae would immediately signal her body that she was in danger and trigger a massive fight or flight response. This was a physical response that needed to be addressed for her to return to a normal life.

Of course, dealing with the physical side of her problem was only part of the solution. As with most physical conditions, there were mental and spiritual issues that also needed to be addressed for a true healing. We will discuss these in the chapters that follow. For now, let's refocus on the physical side of emotions and look at the role emotions play in communication.

EMOTIONS AND COMMUNICATION

Communication is the process of conveying our thoughts and feelings to others. Emotions play an important non-verbal role in communication by adding information to what is being said through subtle variations in tone of voice, facial expressions, posture, and gestures.

Take a moment to say the words "I love you" out loud three times, first as a question, then as a fact, and finally as a passionate affirmation. Notice the changes in your voice, face, and inner feelings as you say these words in each of the three ways. These differences allow a listener to know which meaning you intend to convey without explanation.

The most remarkable thing about this ability to signal meanings emotionally is that you were born with it. How do we know this faculty is inborn? First, people who are born blind have the same basic emotional expressions as people who see. Second, while we can modify our behavior and expressions for weak emotions, strong emotions produce the same basic facial expressions in everyone no matter where they are from.

In addition, research with infants has shown that emotional expression is our first language. This is why parents of young children often find that on days when they are relaxed and in a good mood, their children display their best behavior. On days when parents are frustrated or stressed, children tend to misbehave more. Children are simply responding to their parent's non-verbal communication. Since they are not yet able to make sense out of their parent's stress, they become anxious and act out the tension they perceive. As we learn to use language, we become less conscious of this inborn ability. However, it is this inborn ability to "read" people that can let us know when others are trying to hide something such as emotional pain or when they are trying to deceive us.

This ability to communicate through emotional expression even goes beyond reading other people and extends to animals. It turns out that expressions such as baring your teeth when you are angry can also be seen in dogs, cats, and a host of animals. Many such subtle cues allow pet owners to know how their pets are feeling even though they cannot talk. For example, Pat, a friend of mine, enjoys telling how her dog, Gloria, actually smiles when she is told that she is going for a walk.

THE ROLE OF MEDICATIONS WITH EMOTIONAL PROBLEMS

As you have seen in this chapter, emotions have a definite physical side. In our earnest desire to see lives changed through prayers of faith, we must not forget that emotional problems are sometimes due either wholly or in part to physical problems in the brain. Again, this is simply part of living in a broken world. Just as many people have problems with their vision, some have emotional "wiring" that is not quite right. Now most Christians see no problem with getting glasses to help with flawed vision or taking medication to manage a problem with the thyroid. However, many of the same Christians see the use of medication for emotional problems as a sign of spiritual weakness if not overt sin.

Although medication is not the answer to every problem, and sometimes makes matters worse, there are many situations where it can play a useful and sometimes essential role in helping to manage emotional problems. At the same time, because we live in a world where the "quick fix" is sought by many, it is important to be wise when deciding whether medications can be helpful. Guidelines for seeking help with emotional issues are given at the back of this book in Appendix 3: Suggestions for Seeking Help.

Pointing out that medication can help with some types of emotional problems is not meant to deny or limit God's ability to bring about miraculous healings. He can and does do that. However, it is useful to think about how God usually works with a physical problem such as a broken leg. God has blessed people with wisdom on how to set a broken leg so the healing abilities that we've already been given can return it to a healthy state. In a similar way, God has blessed people with the knowledge and ability to discover medications that can be used with many types of emotional problems. As with other types of medical knowledge, these medications in the hands of wise practitioners are often the means He uses to heal people.

▶RECOMMENDED ACTIVITIES

SPEND TIME WITH GOD

I once heard the following comment in a sermon: "When you get married, you don't turn to your new wife and say, 'See you next Sunday.' What an empty marriage that would be!" Yet this is exactly what many Christians do. Just as married couples need to spend time together if their relationship is to develop any depth, we need to spend time alone with God if we are going to experience the richness and blessings that a dynamic relationship with God can provide.

Jesus is our perfect example of this. The Bible reports on how He would get up "very early in the morning, while it was still dark" and go to a solitary place to pray (Mark 1:35). Sometimes, He would spend the night alone on a mountain side praying (Luke 6:12). His need to be alone and spend time with His Father was especially strong at crucial turning points, such as when John the Baptist was beheaded (Matthew 14:13, 22–23) or when He was preparing to go to the cross (Matthew 26:36–46). Jesus knew His Father's heart, not just because He is a part of the divine Trinity, but because He spent lots of time in communion and fellowship with God.

Prayer takes time and effort but brings many kinds of benefits. If you have a rich prayer life, this is not news to you. However, if you have never spent regular time in prayer or struggle with this basic "spiritual discipline", decide when and where you are going to spend regular time with God. If you are new to prayer and this seems overwhelming or difficult, start with a short time such as ten minutes. Many like to start the day with prayer. If this appeals to you, plan to get up fifteen minutes earlier and find a place in your home where you will not be disturbed.

If you are not sure what you should do, specific suggestions are offered in Appendix 2: Suggestions on How to Develop a Regular Prayer Life at the back of this book. Read it through a few times. Then select and begin using the ideas that fit your lifestyle and personality. If you've never spent regular time in prayer, you will find that a month of regular, earnest prayer will give you an experience of God that you've never had before.

DEEPEN YOUR CONNECTION WITH A CHURCH BODY

The previous chapter discussed the important role that experience plays in both gaining understanding and growth. It also emphasized that fellowship with a body of sincere believers is essential for the Christian walk. If you are now attending only worship services, I cannot stress enough the importance of becoming involved with some type of Bible study or small group. Take a look at your church bulletin, or talk with someone you know at your church, and identify an avenue through which you can fellowship with other church members more personally.

If you are still seeking a church you can belong to, I encourage you to continue your search. That is the only way you will get the most out of this book, and, more important, out of what God has to offer you.

Consider the Physical Side of any Emotional Problem You Might Be Experiencing

If you are experiencing any major type of emotional problem, such as depression or excessive anxiety, and have not ruled out physical factors that could be contributing to it, make an appointment for a physical exam by a doctor. Be sure to tell the doctor all your symptoms and concerns. You may also want to consider going to a therapist who specializes in the type of problem you are experiencing. Be sure to look at Appendix 3: Suggestions for Seeking Help.

Continue to Record Examples of Times when You Experience Strong Emotions

Continue to record in your journal times when you experience strong emotions, either positive or negative. This will provide valuable material for the activities in the chapters that follow. If you have not yet begun to do this, review the guidelines given in the Recommended Activities for chapter 2.

CHAPTER 4

BEING A WISE STEWARD OF YOUR BODY

C hapter 3 gave examples of how physical problems in the body and brain can cause major emotional problems. However, it turns out that any type of illness, fatigue, or stress interferes with the proper functioning of your emotions – the more serious the illness or the greater the fatigue or stress, the greater the interference. This interference tends to exaggerate your emotions and increases the chances that they will lead to actions that both interfere with your life and do not please God. A simple exercise demonstrates this.

Think of a recent time when you were healthy and rested and had little stress in your life. How did you interact with people?

How did you approach routine tasks at home and work? Now think of a recent time when you were ill, fatigued from a heavy workload, or facing a major stressor. How did you interact with people? How did you approach routine tasks? The difference in how you responded both mentally and emotionally to people and events is probably obvious.

While mental and spiritual factors also affect how your emotions function, emotions usually are easiest to manage and function best when you are healthy, rested, and free from stress. Unfortunately, we live in a broken world where there is illness, people tainted by sin, and we earn our living through "painful toil" (Genesis 3:17). Even so, there are three general ways you can improve how your emotions work: being a wise steward of the miraculous body that you have been blessed with; observing Sabbath rest; and learning a few simple ways to manage times of high stress more effectively.

BEING A WISE STEWARD OF YOUR BODY

Paul wrote:

> Do you not know that your body is a temple of the Holy Spirit, who is in you, whom you have received from God? You are not your own; you were bought at a price. Therefore honor God with your body" (1 Corinthians 6:19–20).

Elsewhere, he wrote:

> In him the whole building is joined together and rises to become a holy temple in the Lord. And in him you too are being built together to become a dwelling in which God lives by his Spirit" (Ephesians 2:21–22).

As the temple of the Holy Spirit, your body is meant to be used to glorify God in service and worship and to become an instrument of righteousness:

> I urge you, brothers, in view of God's mercy, to offer your bodies as living sacrifices, holy and pleasing to God — this is your spiritual act of worship" (Romans 12:1).

> Do not offer the parts of your body to sin, as instruments of wickedness, but rather offer yourselves to God, as those who have been brought from death to life; and offer the parts of your body to him as instruments of righteousness (Romans 6:13).

Just as a car will not serve you well if it is not in proper working order, a body that is not working properly interferes with your ability to serve God. Three general health concerns are often neglected in today's world. The first two are the need for a proper diet and regular exercise. These are well-known keys to maintaining health. Since they are both such broad topics and there is a wealth of information already available on them, I will not go into them in detail. However, if you are having difficulty managing some aspect of your emotions, one of the contributing factors may simply be that you are not taking care of yourself in these two areas.

A third health concern that I do want to discuss, which can have a major impact on how your emotions work, is lack of sleep. Several studies have shown that the average person is chronically sleep deprived. The main reason for this is the combination of artificial lighting and the various forms of electronic entertainment that are now available. We often stay up much later than is healthy for us. Here are several common signs that can indicate that you are not getting enough sleep.

- You rely on caffeine to stay awake and alert.
- If you sit quietly for a few minutes without any distractions, you tend to fall asleep.
- You depend on an alarm clock to wake up. If you repeatedly hit the snooze button, this is an even stronger sign.
- You tend to get sleepy when driving.
- You find it hard to concentrate and make mistakes that could be avoided with better concentration.
- You are having trouble with short-term memory and forget things.
- You are moody, depressed, and anxious or you lack patience and become easily frustrated.
- You frequently get sick.

Most adults require seven to eight hours of sleep each night. However, some individuals need as little as five hours or as much as ten hours each night. An easy way to discover your personal sleep requirements is to do the following. Select a period of three or four days when you do not have to get up early for work and you are not sick or facing any major stressors. Go to sleep when you normally do and do not set an alarm clock. Note when you wake up. The length of time you slept is probably your normal requirement. If you are greatly sleep deprived, it may take a few days to find what your normal pattern is because your body will try to "catch up" on missed sleep. You will know that you are getting your normal requirement when you awake feeling refreshed and rested rather than sluggish and tired.

If you cannot do this over several consecutive days, do it over four consecutive weekends. If, after the first two weekend trials, you note that you are sleeping longer on the weekend than during the weekdays, lengthen your weekday sleep period, and see if that changes the last two weekend trials.

SABBATH REST

The fourth commandment states:

> Remember the Sabbath day by keeping it holy. Six days you shall labor and do all your work, but the seventh day is a Sabbath to the LORD your God. On it you shall not do any work, neither you, nor your son or daughter, nor your manservant or maidservant, nor your animals, nor the alien within your gates. For in six days the LORD made the heavens and the earth, the sea, and all that is in them, but he rested on the seventh day. Therefore the LORD blessed the Sabbath day and made it holy. (Exodus 20:8–11)

The above commandment is the longest of all the commandments and includes two reasons for keeping this day of rest. First, God rested on the seventh day and "made it holy." We are to follow the example He gave us. Second, we are to use this time to reflect on the spiritual heritage we have as God's chosen and now freed people. As slaves in Egypt, the Israelites did not enjoy any days off. The idea of rest was new and revolutionary. Moreover, it was a gift from God, just as their freedom was not earned but given to them by God, who used Moses as their deliverer. This foreshadows the gospel message that we have been freed from slavery to sin and given the gift of rest in Christ.

As God continued to instruct Moses in how to make a nation out of a group of slaves who knew nothing of how to act like citizens of a chosen nation, He included many special days of rest, celebration, and remembrance in the form of festivals, sabbatical years and jubilees. We no longer follow the Jewish calendar and tend to look at these traditions as part of the legalism of the Old Testament. However, although the ceremonial laws of Israel have been replaced by the freedom we have in Christ, the basic laws concerning love of God, one's neighbor and oneself have not changed. In fact, they are now extended to include love of one's enemies.

In the same way, the law regarding the Sabbath still stands as the pivotal point between the first three which deal with how we are to love God and no other, and the final six which have to do with loving our neighbors. In many ways, keeping the Sabbath enables us to observe both sets of commandments to love. We need Sabbath rest to be spiritually recharged so we can function as God intended. We also need it to restore our mental and emotional sides.

Since we are physical beings, our bodies need this time to recover from six days of activity. The idea of taking periodic rests between times of work often seems misplaced in our busy schedules. Many people are in constant motion doing things. Even their "rest" is occupied by chores, going someplace, or doing something. When people do stop and take time to refrain from daily tasks, they tend to plug themselves into television, video games, or some other type of electronic diversion filling their heads with anything but peace and rest.

Fortunately, most have schedules that enable them to take their Sabbath rest on Sunday if they would only do so. If you are required to work on Sundays or are so busy in ministry on Sunday that it is your busiest day of the week, you can use an alternate day to rest. The important thing is to begin following the owner's manual that we've been given and perform the routine maintenance that it recommends. If you've never practiced taking a Sabbath rest, do so for a month, and note the difference it makes in your life.

MANAGING EMOTIONS DURING TIMES OF HIGH STRESS

Finally, let's look at the problem of dealing with times of high stress. These might include problems with your mate, deadlines at work, financial difficulties, caring for a sick family member, or dealing with a child who is going through a difficult period and acting out in some way. During times like these you think less clearly and have stronger emotional responses than usual. Here are four guidelines that can help you manage more effectively these periodic times of high stress.

Recognize That You Are in a Period of High Stress

While this might seem obvious, many people do not recognize when stress is affecting their ability to think and act effectively. In fact, many people recognize that they are stressed only when they begin experiencing major negative symptoms. Recognizing the early signs that stress is having a negative effect on you enables you to take action when you are most able to deal with the stress effectively. Just as with a physical illness, the longer you wait to address it, the more difficult it is to overcome.

A simple way to recognize the early signs of stress is to identify specific things that you do only during times of stress. A simple exercise is given in the Recommended Activities that you can use to identify some of these behaviors. Once you've identified a few of these behaviors, they become warning signs that alert you to the need to take the following actions.

Set Priorities

Curious things happen when you are experiencing high levels of stress. One of them is that little things become major issues.

The importance of a small mistake, a delay in traffic, or a small irritating thing that your partner does becomes exaggerated and can trigger strong emotions when you are stressed. These same things tend to be insignificance and trigger little or no emotion when life is calm. This is because you are thinking in a more black-and-white manner, and your emotions have become more exaggerated. Unfortunately, this tendency can cause you to waste your energy and fail to accomplish the important things that you need to focus on.

When you are under stress, take a few moments to identify what you need to do. Some like to make a short list. Then remind yourself that everything else can wait for another day. If you have children, it is especially important to avoid trying to resolve issues about their behavior that concern you when you are stressed. When you are sick, hungry, tired, or facing unusual stress, just stick to the basics and maintain order. Address long-term issues when things are less stressful and you are thinking more calmly and clearly.

As you set priorities, remind yourself that you will probably be more emotional than normal because of the stress that you are experiencing. Because of this it is probably wise to delay dealing with emotional issues until the immediate stress has passed and you are less emotional.

Reduce Activities and Ask for Help
Because stress triggers the fight or flight response, it reduces the overall energy you have. Think of the gas tank in your car. On days when you are rested and relaxed, you have a full tank that you can use to accomplish tasks. On days when you are experiencing high levels of stress, you only have half of a tank. So, part of setting priorities is to reduce and simplify the

number of things you need to do. For example, you might do less cleaning, and prepare simpler meals. If possible, ask others to help with some of the things you normally do. For example, at home you might ask your mate to give you more help with daily chores. Children can take on additional household duties for a short time. At work, a co-worker might be able to help with one of your routine tasks.

Take More Time with Decisions

Because your reasoning ability is diminished and you are more emotional when you are stressed, take more time with decisions. If you have a major decision to make, take a little more time to think about it. It might also be important to discuss it with someone you trust who has good judgment. If you find yourself becoming emotional, take a break and calm down. If possible, delay the decision so you can look at things when you are feeling less stressed.

While each of the suggestions probably seems obvious, the unfortunate reality is that many people do not follow them. They simply don't think of them. If this is true for you, make a copy of these ideas and put them on a wall where you can see them for a few weeks. Having them firmly implanted in the back of your mind increases the chances that you will actually act on them.

▶Recommended Activities

Identify Your "Stress Indicators"

We all have things we do when we are stressed that are not part of our usual behavior. This inventory can help you identify specific behaviors that can alert you to times when stress is interfering with your ability to think clearly and perform routine tasks.

Take a moment now to recall two or three recent times when you've experienced high levels of stress. Now, go through the following list of stress symptoms, and check any that you exhibit during those times which you do not exhibit when you are not stressed.

Common Symptoms Associated with Stress

PHYSICAL

___ Colds, flu, or other minor illness	___ "Nervous" stomach
___ Decreased appetite	___ Rash
___ Headache	___ Sleeplessness
___ Lack of energy, fatigue	___ Teeth grinding
___ Increased appetite	___ Tingling or cold hands or feet
___ Increased problems with allergies, asthma, arthritis, or other chronic physical conditions	___ Weight change: increase or decrease
___ Muscle tension, aches	Other: _____ _____

MENTAL

___ Confusion	___ Racing thoughts
___ Difficulty thinking clearly	___ "Weird" or morbid thoughts
___ Forgetfulness	___ Whirling mind
___ Inability to concentrate	Other:
___ Lack of creativity	_____
___ Lethargy	_____
___ Negative attitude	
___ Poor memory	

EMOTIONAL

___ Anger

___ Anxiety

___ Depression

___ Increased emotionalism

___ Irritability

___ Mood swings

___ Short temper

___ The "blues"

___ Troubled sleep, nightmares

Other:

_____

_____

BEHAVIORAL

___ Difficulty "getting started" on things that need to be done

___ Increase in activities that waste time

___ Frequent sighing, yawning

___ Idleness

___ Increase in mistakes or accidents

___ Increased use of alcohol, tobacco, or other drugs

___ Increased use of profanity, put-downs, or sarcasm

___ Increase in nervous habits: finger-drumming, foot-tapping, etc.

___ Low productivity

Other:

_____

_____

RELATIONAL

___ Blaming

___ Clinginess

___ Decreased or increased sex drive

___ Distrustful

___ Fewer contacts with friends

___ Increased arguments, disagreements

___ Isolation from loved ones and friends

___ Intolerance

___ Lack of intimacy

___ Lashing out

___ Less loving and trusting   ___ Resentful

___ More demanding   Other:

___ Nagging

___ Needy

SPIRITUAL

___ Apathy   ___ Sense of being a martyr

___ Cynicism   ___ Need to "prove" self

___ Doubt   ___ "No one cares" attitude

___ Discouragement   ___ No peace

___ Emptiness   ___ Pessimism

___ Feeling distant from God   ___ Sense of helplessness

___ Inability to forgive   ___ Sense of hopelessness

___ Little joy   Other:

___ Loss of direction

___ Loss of faith

___ Loss of meaning

If you are like most, you probably checked many of the above symptoms. Some, however, are more important indicators than others. Go back through the list, and circle three symptoms that you feel are the most important indicators that stress is beginning to have a negative effect on you. Think of these indicators as being like the warning lights on your car's dashboard. These warning lights let you know when there is a minor problem that needs to be addressed in order for your car to run properly. In the same way, your indicators are simply warning signs that let you know you need to begin using the guidelines mentioned in this chapter to manage this season of high stress more effectively.

Using Your Stress Indicators

After you've completed the Stress Symptom Inventory and identified three indicators, take some time to reflect on times when you have been stressed and answer the following questions:

- How did the stress I was experiencing affect my emotions?
- Did I experience any emotions that I normally do not experience?
- Were my emotions stronger than usual? How so?
- Was there anything that prevented me from setting priorities and focusing on these activities while "letting go" of everything else.
- Was there someone I could have asked to help me? If I didn't, what prevented me from asking for help?
- Should I have delayed or taken more time with certain decisions?
- What could I do in the future when I'm facing this type of stress to use some of the ideas in this chapter?

Be sure to record your responses and insights in your journal.

Practice Taking Sabbath Rests

Plan your Sunday or another day of the week to impose the fewest possible demands on your physical and emotional energies. For example, you can prepare food the day before, go out to eat or have foods you can simply heat and set out. Join others in worship or go where you are able to reflect on God. Be sure to include time to pray for both loved ones as well as others in your life, including those who may be causing difficulties for you. Review the reasons you are reading this book and the insights that God has given you so far. Ask for help in understanding the lessons in a way that will help you become more like the image of Christ. If you are very busy, consider starting with half-day Sabbath rests.

Don't forget that play is an essential part of Sabbath rest. Take time for a movie, sport, music, or anything else that is fun and enjoyable. Sabbath rest should also include time with loved ones. Spend time with friends and family with whom you have positive relationships. As much as possible do only those things which truly restore and revitalize you.

Consider Your Sleep Patterns

This chapter discussed the need for sufficient sleep for your emotions to function properly. Review the common indicators for sleep deprivation. If you checked two or more, do the exercise that was described and determine your normal sleep requirements. Once you've done so, start going to sleep at a time that allows you to get sufficient sleep.

Take a Look at Diet and Exercise

Take some time this week to look at what you eat and how you move. If you are not taking care of yourself, take some time to make a list of three simple things you can do to improve how you eat or include some exercise in your daily life. These can be as simple as eating an apple instead of a candy bar or using the stairs instead of the elevator. If diet or exercise is a major issue for you, talk with someone who is trained in this area.

TAKE SHORT BREAKS AFTER TIMES OF INTENSE ACTIVITY

One extension of the idea of Sabbath rest is to include short breaks in your daily schedule. Many people plunge from one activity into another. They do not allow time for the mind and body to recover in between. If this describes you, take time for short breaks after times of intense activity. This allows your body to relax and often makes a big difference in how you respond to people and events emotionally.

If you often work through your morning, afternoon, and lunch breaks, begin to take them. Most find that taking time to unwind and break from work actually makes them more productive. If you work at home, set specific times to stop and relax for a few minutes.

After work or a stressful day, develop a ritual or routine you can use to unwind. Many people find that a solitary activity such as reading, working at a relaxing hobby, or just sitting is effective. Others prefer activities involving children, spouses, or friends. This does not need to be long or drawn out. Often, ten to twenty minutes is enough to reenergize you and put you on an emotional even keel.

CHAPTER 5

THE MENTAL SIDE OF EMOTIONS

T he Bible is filled with passages that acknowledge the importance of our ability to think and reason. Isaiah 1:18 invites us "Come now, let us reason together." Paul urges us to "be transformed by the renewing of your mind" (Romans 12:2) and points out that the spiritual person will be found to have the "mind of Christ" (1 Corinthians 2:16). The psalmist cries out, "Teach me your decrees" (119:12, 68). The opening of Proverbs is devoted to the importance of gaining wisdom. When meeting with the disciples after his resurrection, Jesus "opened their minds so they could understand the Scriptures" (Luke 24:45). This is but a small sampling of verses that demonstrate the important role that your thoughts and beliefs play in your life. This is especially true with your emotions.

In this and the next chapter, we explore the mental aspect of emotions by looking at what is known as the cognitive model of emotions. This model describes the relationship between your thoughts and the various emotions you experience. Understanding this relationship will give you a deeper understanding and appreciation of Scriptures such as those listed above. The model also underscores important biblical principles for managing your emotions more effectively and transforming them so they function more nearly as they were intended to function when Adam and Eve were first created.

THE COGNITIVE MODEL OF EMOTIONS

The word "cognition" refers to thought. Thus the cognitive model of emotions focuses on the role that thoughts play in generating emotions. In its simplest terms, this model sees your emotions as a response to your perception of events and the meaning you assign to them. When something happens, your mind uses both conscious and unconscious mental processes to arrive at an interpretation of the event. It is this interpretation that triggers the emotions you experience. In turn, these emotions then urge you to act in line with your interpretation of the event. This process is usually diagrammed as follows:

Event ⟶ Interpretation ⟶ Emotion ⟶ Action

Because many of your emotions are generated by your perception and interpretation of events, common statements such as "You made me angry" and "That made me sad" are inaccurate. It is not the person or event that makes you angry or sad but your interpretation of it.

The story of David's encounter with King Saul described in 1 Samuel 24 is a good illustration of how different interpretations can trigger widely divergent emotional responses. Saul was told that

David was in the Desert of En Gedi and pursued him with three thousand chosen men. While David and his men were hiding far back in a cave, Saul went into it to relieve himself. David's men were excited: they saw this as an opportunity to kill Saul. David saw things differently. He crept up and cut off a corner of Saul's robe without his noticing it. Afterwards, his men were angry because they saw this as a lost chance to eliminate someone who was threatening their lives. However, David "was conscience-stricken for having cut off a corner of [Saul's] robe. He said to his men, 'The LORD forbid that I should do such a thing to my master, the Lord's anointed, or lift my hand against him; for he is the anointed of the LORD'" (1 Samuel 24:5–6). The same circumstances, interpreted differently, resulted in utterly dissimilar emotions in David from those of his men.

When we look more closely at the various interpretations that generate emotions, we find that they are based on whether a need has been satisfied, a threat has been perceived, or a loss has occurred. In this simplified model, the satisfaction of a need triggers the various positive emotions such as joy, satisfaction, and excitement. A threat triggers anger or fear. A loss triggers sadness. Keep in mind that as the words anger, fear and sadness are used here, each represents a broad range of emotions. Anger can range from irritation to rage, fear can range from apprehension to panic, and sadness can range from disappointment to deep depression. This expanded cognitive model can be diagrammed as follows:

While most of our emotions are generated through the cognitive process described above, there are some important exceptions. Chapter 3 showed that many physical things can interfere with your emotional mechanism such as drugs, chemical toxins, and inherited traits that cause chemical imbalances as well as everyday hunger, fatigue, illness, and stress. In addition, some emotional responses seem to be "hard wired" into us, like the excitement felt when seeing an attractive member of the opposite sex. Another important type of emotional response that does not fit the above cognitive model is something called a conditioned emotional response which is explored in chapter 10.

HOW BELIEFS AFFECT YOUR INTERPRETATION OF EVENTS

Many influences shape the way you interpret events. The one that is easiest to become aware of is your beliefs. The beliefs that you hold are a primary resource that the mind uses to decide whether something is safe, dangerous, desirable, or unimportant. As described above, these interpretations then generate emotions that urge you to take action. If you believe that something is dangerous, you avoid it or attack it. If you believe it is desirable, you try to obtain it. If you believe it is unimportant, you ignore it. The more strongly you believe something, the stronger are the emotion and the consequent urge to take action based on that belief.

Looking again at the example of David and his men described in 1 Samuel, we see that David's men saw Saul as an enemy who needed to be destroyed. As such, their desire was to kill Saul and eliminate the threat he posed. This is why they were so angry when he escaped. David, however, saw Saul as "the LORD's anointed." His belief in this and his devotion to God were so strong that they far exceeded the threat that Saul posed. As such, he was duty bound to do no harm to Saul since to do so would be to go against the will of God. This is why David would not harm his king and why he was conscious stricken after cutting off a corner of Saul's robe when he could have made his point without doing so.

This connection between your beliefs and the emotions you experience provides an important key for understanding why emotions become so destructive when they, like everything else that God created, were intended to be a blessing. Interpretations that are based on worldly beliefs rather than reflecting the mind of God generate emotions such as anxiety, fear, hate, anger, resentment, jealousy, and envy. This is why it is essential to know and understand the Bible if you want your emotions to function as God intended them to function.

As you come to know and understand God's Word, you find that your interpretation of events begins to fall more and more in line with the way God sees both you and the world. This, in turn, triggers emotions that are more in line with what pleases God. Understanding the forgiveness that you've been granted makes it easier to forgive others when you've been wronged and compassion replaces anger. When you see someone who is proud and arrogant, instead of feeling defensive or irritated, you feel sadness when you realize how lost this person is. As you experience the patience that God has had with you, you find it easier to be patient with others. As you experience how God truly does love you and has a glorious future awaiting you, peace and joy replace worry and fear.

Understanding the temporary nature of this life and having confidence in both the resurrection and our future with Christ allows us to conquer the most terrifying of fears: death. This allows Christians facing death to experience a peace that the world doesn't understand and proclaim boldly with Paul: "Where, O death, is your victory? Where, O death, is your sting?" (1 Corinthians 15:55). This confidence also allows boldness to replace fear when talking about Christ with others.

Before going on, let's pause for a moment and take a closer look at two words that I have used in the previous paragraphs: *know* and *understand*. To know something is to be aware of it and have information about it. To understand something is to know it thoroughly as a result of close contact or long experience with it. One of the problems with looking at the cognitive aspect of emotions is that people often believe that simply learning information is all that is required to change the way you behave and react emotionally. While "renewing your mind" is important, the other dimensions that we've been looking at — subjective, physical, and mental — are just as important.

The role of experience in shaping your beliefs and emotional reactions offers a good example of how true understanding requires more than just knowledge. Chapter 2 discussed how experience puts an emotional "stamp" on some of the information you have learned making it more important than information that lacks this stamp. So while *knowing* your Bible is important, spending time with God in prayer and meditation and spending time with God's people is how you come to *understand* what God's Word is saying. These experiences give the words you have read an emotional stamp that makes them come alive and provide true understanding. It is this understanding that causes true changes in how you interpret daily events and in how you respond to events emotionally. One of the best examples of knowledge without understanding can be found in the book of James where it says, "You believe that there is one God. Good! Even the demons believe that — and shudder" (James 2:19). Demons know that there is one God, but they do not understand Him.

HOW HABITS AFFECT YOUR INTERPRETATION OF EVENTS

Although we often make conscious decisions about what an event means and how we should respond, many of our emotional responses and behaviors are simply ingrained habits. Chapter 3 discussed how the mind is a symphony of activity, most of which is going on outside our awareness. Some behaviors become so automatic that we need very little conscious attention to carry them out. Let's take a simple example: brushing your teeth. This is something most of us do with hardly any conscious thought. The next time you brush your teeth, hold the brush with the opposite hand from the one you normally use. Note how much mental effort is needed to perform a task that usually requires very little thought.

Just as how you brush your teeth is a simple habit pattern, the way you think about and interpret everyday events is a mental habit pattern. As you grew, you learned to identify different objects, people, and events as safe or dangerous, desirable or unimportance. Your brain then associated an emotion with each, such as excitement, fear, desire, or no emotion. Each object, person, or event now triggers your rehearsed mental, behavioral, and emotional responses when encountered. The curious thing is that these responses often clash with what we say we believe. However, since we are responding with little or no conscious thought, we often don't even realize that there is a conflict.

Modern electronic media such as television, movies, the Internet, and video games play an important role in developing and maintaining these associations. People who spend a lot of time viewing graphic images and stories with anger, violence, and sexual content are mentally rehearsing corresponding mental and emotional responses. The more you rehearse a given set of responses, the more likely you are to find yourself acting them out in real life situations.

This does not mean that watching violent movies is going to make you into a serial killer. However, numerous studies have indicated that it will cause you to become more aggressive. Likewise, watching programs loaded with sexual content tends to cause you to dwell on sexual thoughts and focus more on the sexual aspect of members of the opposite sex. This is one of the reasons that Paul exhorts you "Whatever is true, whatever is noble, whatever is right, whatever is pure, whatever is lovely, whatever is admirable — if anything is excellent or praiseworthy — think about such things" (Philippians 4:8). Doing this causes your brain to attach value to those things that are true, noble, right, pure, lovely, admirable, excellent, and praiseworthy. Sadly, we often spend too much time thinking about and immersing ourselves in things that are just the opposite. Indeed, much of the modern secular world of advertising and entertainment reinforces attitudes, beliefs, and behaviors that are opposite from those that God wants us to develop.

Take a moment to consider the worldview and beliefs that underlie the commercials and programs you've watched and the secular material you have read recently. Put a check mark by any of the following ideas that were expressed:

____ We are here to enjoy the "good life".

____ We should not have to deny ourselves the things we want.

____ Personal restraint is neither necessary nor good. If it feels good, do it.

____ We have a right to happiness.

____ Life should always be fun and exciting.

____ Stay with your partner only as long as it is enjoyable; then find someone new.

___ Nobody should have to suffer or endure anything unpleasant.

___ Life should be fair.

___ We should not have to think deeply or struggle with difficult ideas.

___ We shouldn't have to wait for what we want.

___ There is no absolute truth, nor is there any absolute right or wrong. Everything is relative.

___ There are many ways in which one can be spiritual and find God. All are equally valid.

___ Duty, honor, and service are old-fashioned concepts that keep you from enjoying life.

___ It's okay to cheat, lie, and steal if circumstances warrant it. Everyone does it.

___ Sex is a natural function and has no moral implications as long as you don't spread disease or fail to prevent conception. Enjoy it as much as you can.

___ Consenting adults have the right to do whatever they want in private.

___ Marriage is just a formality.

___ Most of our problems are "scars" inflicted on us by religion, parents, or society.

___ Guilt and shame are harmful and may be symptoms of psychological illness.

___ You're maladjusted if the fear of God keeps you from doing something you might enjoy.

While these are all common messages in the modern world of advertising and entertainment, they are all directly opposed to the truths that God has spoken to us in the Bible. They are what Paul refers to as "the wisdom of this world" (1 Corinthians 3:19) and a "worldly point of view" (2 Corinthians 5:16). James describes this as a false "wisdom" which, he points out, "does not come down from heaven but is earthly, unspiritual, of the devil" (3:15). Whenever your thoughts or actions are based on the world's "wisdom," you have "exchanged the truth of God for a lie" (Romans 1:25).

THE FATHER OF LIES

Satan goes by many different names. Each describes a particular aspect of his personality. We see one of these aspects in John 8:44 where Jesus says, "When he lies, he speaks his native language, for he is a liar and the father of lies." One of Satan's strategies has been to implant lies like those listed above into the world that generate emotions and behaviors that separate us from God and cause all kinds of pain and sorrow.

Satan's work of implanting lies into the human consciousness began with Adam and Eve and continues today. As with them, some of his lies simply foster doubt about God's intentions and trustworthiness: "Did God really say, 'You must not eat from any tree in the garden'?" (Genesis 3:1). Others are more direct and encourage us to become our own god: "For God knows that when you eat of it your eyes will be opened, and you will be like God, knowing good and evil" (Genesis 3:5). Indeed, the desire to make ourselves god instead of honoring the true God and keeping Him in His in rightful place as the Lord of our lives is one of the most basic elements of our sinful nature.

As the sons and daughters of Adam and Eve multiplied and spread over the world, Satan continued his work and today there are many lies that permeate our society. Most are based on two fundamental lies. The first is the idea that God has little or no influence in our day-to-day lives because He does not exist, is not interested in us or is far removed from everyday life. The second is that this life is all you've got. Indeed, the secular beliefs listed in the previous section are all logical extensions of these two lies.

THE TRUTH WILL SET YOU FREE

The key to challenging the lies that Satan has spread so effectively in the world and freeing yourself from their effects is to learn the truth and practice living it. John's Gospel reports Jesus' saying to the Jews who had believed him: "If you hold to my teaching, you are really my disciples. Then you will know the truth, and the truth will set you free" (8:31–32). The more you know and understand the truths of the Bible, the easier it is to identify the lies of the world. As you identify specific lies that are driving your thoughts and behaviors, practice telling yourself the truth. As the truth replaces the lie, you will find that your emotions change because you are now seeing things as God sees them. This, in turn, helps you to act in new and more Christlike ways.

Whenever you identify a lie that is holding you in bondage in some area of your life, three measures can help you change it. First, ask God to both help you see when this lie is controlling your thoughts and behavior and fill you with His thoughts. Be sure also to ask God to help with the next two steps.

The second step is to identify Bible verses you can use to counter the lies. If you are not familiar with the Bible, ask for help with this from your pastor or a fellow believer who is mature in Christ and well versed in the Bible. Some find that reference works such as *Nave's Topical Bible*, *Strong's Exhaustive Concordance*, or *Treasury of Scriptural Knowledge* are helpful. There are also several good free Bible search tools available on the Internet.

The third step is to ask someone you trust and who is strong in

Christ to be an accountability partner. Having a person with whom to share one's progress and setbacks has long proved to be effective in strengthening a person's ability to change. Be sure to ask this person to pray for you concerning the thoughts and behaviors you are working to change. A lie that is holding you in bondage will have a spiritual dimension because our battle is not just against a fleshly brain. This is discussed more fully beginning in chapter 7.

►RECOMMENDED ACTIVITIES

IDENTIFY LIES THAT ARE PART OF YOUR BELIEFS AND THINKING

Take a moment to ask God to help you use this exercise to become aware of the lies He want you to see that have been part of your beliefs. Then take some time to think about the past few weeks and identify events that triggered negative emotions such as anger, anxiety, sadness, hurt, jealousy, or resentment. These might include times when others teased, challenged, or hurt you; times when you didn't get what you wanted; or times when something very impersonal happened such as being stuck in traffic or experiencing bad weather. List them on a sheet of paper along with a few words describing what you felt and any thoughts you can recall for each. If you've been recording times when you have been upset in your journal as suggested previously in the recommended activities, you can use that record.

When you are done, identify times when you experienced positive emotions such as excitement, joy, or a deep sense of peace. Again, include a few words describing what you felt and thought with each time you list. Add to your list as you notice new examples during the next few days.

Once you have completed your list, review the list of lies given in the chapter and identify any that might have contributed to the emotions, either negative or positive, that you experienced. As you add new items, review the list again and identify lies that contributed to your reaction.

Since it is impossible to list all the possible lies you may encounter in a short list like the one in this chapter, be aware of other lies that might be part of your thinking. The basic principle is this: Any belief or thought that does not reflect truth as revealed in the Bible is a lie. Whenever you identify a lie that has played a role in the way you have interpreted events that is not on the list in this chapter, be sure to record it in your journal.

For each lie that you identify as being part of your belief system or habitual thinking, write in your own words a simple statement of the truth as presented in the Bible. Then find verses that reflect this truth and use them to expose the lie.

In the following, I have selected ten common lies from the list in the chapter and for each one provided an example of a simple statement of biblical truth that counters it. I've also listed several verses that can be used to replace the lie with the truth whenever you notice it playing a role in your thinking. Keep in mind that the following examples are only meant to be a starting point. A whole book could be written on just this subject. Also, several people who are countering the same lie might use different words to state biblical truth or find that other verses speak more powerfully to them.

Talk to fellow believers as you develop this statement of truth to ensure that you are accurate in your summary of what the Bible says. You may be surprised at the insights that God can speak to you through them which you need to hear. They might also have suggestions on verses which might not occur to you that you will find useful. Don't forget to have others lift you up in prayer as you work to challenge worldly thinking that has hindered your walk.

Lie #1: We are here to enjoy the "good life".
Truth: We were created to please God. He clearly revealed
what pleases Him in the Bible: to worship and serve him.
In doing this we find our ultimate purpose and joy.

Micah 6:8; Matthew 6:25–34; Mark 8:34–35; Romans
8:29; Ephesians 2:10; 1 Thessalonians 4:1; James 1:2–3;
1 John 2:15–17

Lie #2: Personal restraint is neither necessary nor good.
Truth: Self-control is a frequently mentioned virtue in the
Bible. It is also a fruit of the Spirit. It is not only a mark
of maturity, but essential if we are going to act in ways
that please God.

Proverbs 19:2, 25:28; Galatians 5:22–23; 1 Thessalonians
5:6; 1 Timothy 3:2; Titus 2:11–14; 1 Peter 1:13; 2 Peter
1:5–8

Lie #3: We have a right to happiness.
Truth: This is a very big topic. In short, we have no rights,
but we do have privileges as members of God's family.
We find true happiness by serving and worshiping God.
Here are several verses that touch on these ideas:

Ecclesiastes 7:20; Isaiah 53:6; 55:9; Jeremiah 18:1–11; John
9:20–21; 13:12–17; 15:18–20; Galatians 5:13; Ephesians
3:12–13; Philippians 2:5–11; 4:12–14; 1 John 3:1

Lie #4: Nobody should have to suffer or endure anything
unpleasant.
Truth: We live in a world that is broken and tainted by sin.
Because of this we will face hardships. If we follow Christ

faithfully, we will face persecution. We will also experience God's peace and strength in the midst of troubles.

Genesis 3:16–19; Matthew 5:10–11; John 16:33; Romans 8:22–23; 1 Corinthians 10:13; 2 Corinthians 1:3–4; Hebrews 12:7–11; James 1:2–3; 1 Peter 3:17; 4:12–14

Lie #5: We shouldn't have to wait for what we want.
Truth: Patience is a frequently mentioned virtue in the Bible. It is also a fruit of the Holy Spirit. We need to trust that God knows our true desires and meets them as we are ready for them.

Psalm 37:4; Proverbs 19:2; 21:5; Ecclesiastes 7:8; Lamentations 3:26; Matthew 6:31–33; Galatians 5:22–23; Hebrews 6:15; 12:1; James 5:7–8; 10–11; 2 Peter 1:6

Lie #6: There is no absolute truth nor is there any absolute right or wrong. Everything is relative.
Truth: There are absolute truths in this world: God exists; He is a personal God Who has told us in the Bible His plans for the world and what He wants from us; He loves us deeply and has provided a way to draw close to Him through Christ; the Holy Spirit gives us the means by which we can be transformed into what He wants us to be and be blessed.

Genesis 1:1; Psalm 14:1; 19:7–10; Proverbs 14:12; 16:25; 26:12; John 14:6; Romans 1:18–20, 6–23

Lie #7: Sex is a natural function and has no moral implications as long as you don't spread disease or fail to prevent conception. Enjoy it as much as you can.

Truth: Sex is a wonderful gift that needs to be expressed within the limits that God has set for it. Becoming overly focused on sex and pursuing sexual gratification outside of God's guidelines harms us and keeps us from enjoying the truly good things that God wants for us.

Genesis 2:18–25; Ecclesiastes 9:9; Proverbs 18:22; Matthew 19:5–6; 15:19–20; Romans 13:13; 1 Corinthians 6:9; 6:18–20; Ephesians 5:3; Hebrews 12:16

Lie #8: Most of our problems are "scars" inflicted on us by religion, parents, or society.

Truth: While the sinfulness of others and the evil that is in the world do affect us, our basic problem is sin and its effect: separation from God. Once this is resolved through Christ, the Holy Spirit can lead us into true healing as we yield to Him.

Ecclesiastes 7:20; Isaiah 53:6; 59:2; Romans 3:23; 5:12, 8:1–2, Galatians 5:16; James 1:13–15

Lie #9: Guilt and shame are harmful and may be symptoms of psychological illness.

Truth: Guilt and shame do sometimes come from mistaken beliefs about oneself. However, guilt and shame were meant to be a safety regulator the conscience uses to help us distinguish between right and wrong. The Holy Spirit uses them to convict us when we are doing things that are not pleasing to God.

Genesis 4:6–7; Matthew 27:3; John 16:8; Acts 24:16; 2 Corinthians 7:10–11; 1 Timothy 4:2; Titus 1:15; 1 Peter 3:15–16

Lie #10: You're maladjusted if the fear of God keeps you from doing something you might enjoy.

Truth: There are many sinful activities that offer momentary pleasure. However, all sin leads to pain and suffering in the long run. Just as a parent's rules are designed to keep a child safe, God's limits both keep us from harm and lead to true peace and joy.

Proverbs 1:7; 9:10; 15:33; 1 Corinthians 6:12; 9:24; 10:23–24; 2 Corinthians 8:21; Galatians 6:9; 2 Thessalonians 3:13; 1 John 3:10

WHAT ARE YOU CHOOSING FOR ENTERTAINMENT?

Pause to consider what you do with your free time. What types of programs do you watch? What types of music do you listen to? What types of reading material do you enjoy? Where and with whom do you spend your time? Evaluate each in terms of Paul's admonition:

Whatever is true, whatever is noble, whatever is right, whatever is pure, whatever is lovely, whatever is admirable — if anything is excellent or praiseworthy — think about such things (Philippians 4:8).

Ask God to help you see if you need to make any changes. If you decide that you do need to make some changes, be sure to ask God to change your desires and appetites in this area of your life. It also helps if you have an accountability partner you can talk to about what you've discovered and the changes you want to make.

CHAPTER 6

CORE BELIEFS

When Claudia came for counseling sessions, she would wear dark and dowdy clothes. She rarely smiled. When she did, it was a painful smile that pressed through a rock hard exterior.

Claudia grew up in a home where she experienced physical and verbal abuse. Her older brother would call her "dog" and often beat her up. Her mother and father, both alcoholics, were equally abusive both verbally and physically. After graduating from high school, she entered the army and married a man who continued the physical and verbal abuse. However, one day when he hit the older of their two young children, her protective instincts kicked in and she divorced him and moved away.

Claudia had been introduced to Christ as a child and felt a need to reconnect with the only source of solace she had ever known. Unfortunately, she joined a small Christian group run by a man who greatly twisted the gospel for his own ends. Her shame and worthlessness were exploited by this group until one day she could bear it no more. She broke away and joined a mainstream church that proclaimed the true gospel of God's mercy and forgiveness through Christ.

Claudia suffered from depression that had a clear biological basis. She was seeing a good psychiatrist, but like many with this type of depression, she found that the emotional damage from her abusive background intertwined with her biological makeup and made it very difficult for her to experience any joy. She came to me to work on the many psychological issues that plagued her.

After working with Claudia for several weeks and making some progress, I was privileged to see the Holy Spirit do a mighty work in her life. After opening with prayer for her to be delivered from the lies that had held her in bondage all her life, we began exploring the deep sense of worthlessness she felt. As she began to recall the many times she had been told how unlovable and useless she was, I began to share Scriptures that explained how these were lies and how precious she was to God. Suddenly, her eyes were opened, and she asked through tears, "Does God really love me?" With much emotion and a presence of the Holy Spirit that we both felt, I said yes. Through tears of revelation, she quietly began to repeat to herself, "He really does love me!" We closed with a prayer thanking God for the truth that she was able to see and asked that this truth become more real to her than any of the lies that had bound her for so many years.

The next week she came to her appointment wearing a bright yellow flower-print dress and a radiant smile. Anyone who had seen her previously would have known at once that this was a new woman. From that time on she found her life unfolding in new and wonderful ways. She still found that she needed medication to control the biological aspect of her depression, and she still had many issues to work through. However, the remarkable change in how she looked reflected the work that God was doing in her life.

In chapter 5 we looked at how Satan's lies in the form of worldly beliefs lead to interpretations of our experience that separate us from God and generate much of our pain and suffering. In this chapter we go deeper and look at core beliefs that form the center of your being.

Claudia exemplifies how a fundamental change in a destructive core belief can affect how you interpret daily events and make a dramatic change in both the emotions you experience and the way you behave.

CORE BELIEFS

You have a host of beliefs about all aspects of life. These range from the trivial, such as which brand of toothpaste is best, to the profound such as who you are or the nature of God. While beliefs are often seen as something that we have consciously chosen, the various unconscious processes we have discussed in previous chapters often play an important role in shaping them. A good example of this is the type of car that you think is best for you.

When you plan to buy a new car, your decision is based on many unconscious as well as conscious factors. You might read reviews of various cars to see what experts have to say about them and ask opinions of others whom you feel are knowledgeable. However, your final decision is also influenced by experiences you have had with cars in the past and beliefs you have about who you are and your place in the world. These experiences trigger unconscious associations with the various cars you see. Sometimes the responses are subtle, like the influence of images and associations from advertising. Sometimes they are quite strong, as when you see a vehicle and suddenly recall one that had special meaning for you while growing up. In addition, other beliefs and habitual ways of thinking, such as whether you need a "cool" car or a practical one, will influence the final decision you come to.

Sometimes habitual ways of thinking and unconscious factors are in conflict with what you say you believe. For example, if you had asked Claudia about how God viewed her prior to her breakthrough, she would have said that God loved her and that through her faith in Christ she was special in His sight. However, the habitual self-talk and conditioned emotional responses from her childhood often caused her to act and think as if she had no value and deserved the scorn of others—a message that she had been given in many different ways over the years and was now a deeply entrenched part of her identity. These unconscious responses can be seen as a set of rules that we will call core beliefs that controlled Claudia's interpretation of events and behavior in many everyday situations.

The unconscious rules we are describing are not always beliefs in the traditional sense. However, as with Claudia, they often play a major role in shaping one's thoughts and behavior. Another way of looking at these unconscious patterns is to consider the old adage that says, "If it looks like a duck, talks like a duck, and walks like a duck, it's probably a duck." With core beliefs in mind, we can restate this adage: "If you act as if you believe something, speak as if you believe something, and think as if you believe something, you believe it." By labeling these automatic behavioral and thinking patterns as core beliefs, you gain a tool for both thinking about them and changing them.

In Claudia's case, she looked, thought, and acted like she was unlovable. This was a message that she had been given first as a child, then as a wife, then as a member of the abusive sect. So although she had learned that God's nature was love and that she was precious, her thoughts and behavior were largely controlled at a deeper level by the message that she was unlovable.

To be sure, for many people, the core beliefs reflected in their behavior match what they say they believe. However, even when this is true, the idea of core beliefs provides a tool for changing unbiblical emotional responses and behaviors.

It is also true that people whose core beliefs are in conflict with their stated beliefs often are aware of this discrepancy. There were many times in our early work when Claudia would say that she felt worthless and unlovable. At one level, she believed that God loved her, but her emotional reactions were pointing to the destructive core belief that was controlling much of her life. Indeed, as with Claudia, you will find that your emotional reaction to events reveals the core beliefs that direct your life.

The core beliefs that govern much of your behavior and your emotional life can be divided into four basic groups. These include beliefs about:

- Yourself: your personality, strengths, and weaknesses
- The nature of relationships
- The world around you, and
- The nature of God.

The common lies we looked at in chapter 5 mainly dealt with the nature of relationships and the world as viewed by the advertising, entertainment, and popular culture that surrounds us. While these often become an important part of the core beliefs that drive a person's behavior, the destructive core beliefs we are looking at in this chapter usually arise from the experiences you had while growing up.

During childhood, there are many things that can cause people to develop destructive core beliefs where they see themselves as being inadequate, undeserving, worthless, or incompetent. One common source is primary caregivers who are overly harsh, unloving, negative, abusive, absent, or immature. However, children in good homes with loving parents can also develop negative core beliefs. Sometimes this is due to life circumstances such as their parents divorcing, the presence of a disability, or difficulties at school. Emotional or physical trauma can also generate destructive core beliefs such as being the object of derision from other children or abusive interactions with adults outside the family.

Common examples of the types of destructive core beliefs that can plague an individual are listed below. They have been grouped into the four key areas listed above. As you read through them, place a check mark beside any that reflect ideas that you've thought or said or that reflect how you have felt about yourself or your circumstances.

Examples of Destructive Core Beliefs about Yourself

___ I'm inferior to others — I'm not as intelligent, attractive, or capable in some way as others.

___ I'm worthless.

___ I'm unlovable.

___ I'm not interesting or desirable.

___ I'm dirty.

___ My needs are unimportant or bad.

___ I'm a bad person.

___ I can't succeed.

___ I can't do anything right.

___ I'm incompetent.

___ I'm crazy.

___ Anger is dangerous and causes you to lose control (therefore, you must suppress it).

___ Emotions are dangerous, keep them under control or

something bad might happen.

___ My only worth comes from caring for others.

___ My only worth comes from performing, from accomplishing things that are valuable.

___ I don't have the right to protect myself.

___ I can't trust my own feelings or perceptions.

___ It's selfish to have my needs met.

___ My happiness is all that matters.

___ I need to stay in control.

___ I need to always be strong.

___ I am better than others.

___ I can figure things out by myself.

___ I know everything that I need to know.

Examples of Destructive Core Beliefs about Relationships

___ Intimacy is painful (or dangerous), so don't get close.

___ If I get close to someone, I will be hurt.

___ Conflict is dangerous.

___ People aren't reliable; they'll always let you down.

___ You can't trust anyone.

___ Others are in control of my life.

___ Sooner or later, people always abandon you.

___ The only one you can depend on is yourself.

___ In many ways others are my adversaries. I must always be on guard and fight to make sure no one takes what is mine.

___ People in authority are dangerous.

___ No one can understand me.

___ I can lose those I love at any minute.

___ The opposite sex is inferior/superior.

___ I am responsible for others' well-being.

___ I'm responsible for how others feel.

___ If people see how I don't measure up, they will not like me.

___ If you offend others or upset them, they'll abandon you.

___ I must keep the peace and not make others angry or upset with me.

___ I must never do anything that hurts others (even when I am hurt or harmed).

___ It's wrong and selfish to refuse the requests of others.

___ I am entitled to have and do what I want no matter what.

___ I don't need anyone or anything. I can take care of myself.

___ If I allow anyone else to be in charge or have power, I will be harmed.

Examples of Destructive Core Beliefs about the World

___ The world is frightful and dangerous.

___ I'm not safe — something bad can happen at any moment.

___ There is no safe place in the world.

___ When bad things happen to me, it's my fault.

___ I have no power or control.

___ There's nothing I can do to make a difference in how events turn out.

___ Life is meaningless.

___ Life is hard. To live is to suffer.

___ Only the strong survive. Never show weakness.

___ Illness and death are awful. Keep a close watch on your

body because it is weak and fragile and something terrible can go wrong at any time.

___ Winning is everything, losing is for losers.

___ Happiness comes from having things. (Common variations: happiness comes from having power, money,
position, etc.)

Examples of Destructive Core Beliefs about the Nature of God

___ There is no God.

___ God is distant and doesn't interfere with daily life.

___ You create your own destiny — God watches from afar.

___ God doesn't care about me.

___ What I've done is too awful for God to ever love me.

___ God waits for me to sin so He can punish me.

___ God causes bad things to happen.

___ God's love is conditional; it is based on how good we
are/how well we obey His commands.

___ I need to be perfect to please God.

___ I need to be selfless — to never think of myself or my
needs — to please God.

___ God helps those who help themselves.

___ God has already chosen those who will go to heaven
with Him, and we cannot change His mind.

___ If good things happen to you it's because God is happy
with you; if bad things happen to you it's because God
is angry with you.

___ God has favorites.

Just as negative childhood experiences can promote destructive
core beliefs, positive childhood experiences in a home where God

is honored can promote the development of biblical core beliefs that match Scripture and help you live a life that is both satisfying and pleasing to God. In fact, an opposite biblical core belief could be listed for each of the above destructive core beliefs. Here are several examples of destructive core beliefs followed by their opposite biblical core beliefs. Examples of Scripture that supports each biblical core belief are also listed.

> *Destructive core belief:* I'm inferior to others.
> *Opposite biblical core belief:* God made me just as I am
> supposed to be. I have the same value as others in His sight.
>
> Just as each of us has one body with many members,
> and these members do not all have the same function,
> so in Christ we who are many form one body, and each
> member belongs to all the others. (Romans 12:4–5)
>
> For we were all baptized by one Spirit into one body —
> whether Jews or Greeks, slave or free — and we were all
> given the one Spirit to drink . . . so that there should be
> no division in the body, but that its parts should have
> equal concern for each other. (1 Corinthians 12:13, 25)
>
> God has arranged the parts in the body, every one of
> them, just as he wanted them to be. (1 Corinthians 12:18)
>
> *Destructive core belief:* I'm worthless.
> *Opposite biblical core belief:* God sees me as exceedingly
> valuable.
>
> Life is more than food, and the body more than clothes.
> Consider the ravens: They do not sow or reap, they have
> no storeroom or barn; yet God feeds them. And how
> much more valuable you are than birds! (Luke 12:23–24)

God so loved the world that he gave his one and only Son that whoever believes in him shall not perish but have eternal life. (John 3:16)

He chose us in him before the creation of the world to be holy and blameless in his sight. In love he predestined us to be adopted as his sons through Jesus Christ, in accordance with his pleasure and will. (Ephesians 1:4–5)

Destructive core belief: Intimacy is painful (or dangerous), so don't get close.
Opposite biblical core belief: We were made to have intimate relationships with Christ and with others.

The LORD God said, "It is not good for the man to be alone. I will make a helper suitable for him." (Genesis 2:18)

He who finds a wife finds what is good and receives favor from the Lord. (Proverbs 18:22)

A new command I give you: Love one another. As I have loved you, so you must love one another. By this all men will know that you are my disciples, if you love one another. (John 13:34–35)

For his Spirit joins with our spirit to affirm that we are God's children. (Romans 8:16)

Destructive core belief: You can't trust anyone. Sooner or later, people always abandon you.
Opposite biblical core belief: I can trust God. He cares for me and will always be with me. While people are imperfect,

there are people who are trustworthy. I need to learn how to identify them.

Even though I walk through the valley of the shadow of death, I will fear no evil, for you are with me; your rod and your staff, they comfort me. (Ps 23:4)

I am always with you; you hold me by my right hand. You guide me with your counsel, and afterward you will take me into glory. (Psalms 73:23–24)

You came near when I called you, and you said, "Do not fear." (Lamentations 3:57)

Destructive core belief: The world is frightful and dangerous.
Opposite biblical core belief: God will equip me with what I need to manage the problems of this world.

Even though I walk through the valley of the shadow of death, I will fear no evil, for you are with me; (Psalm 23:4)

The Lord is my light and my salvation — whom shall I fear? The LORD is the stronghold of my life — of whom shall I be afraid? (Psalm 27:1)

If God is for us, who can be against us? (Romans 8:29b)

So we say with confidence, "The Lord is my helper; I will not be afraid. What can man do to me?" (Psalm 118:6, Hebrews 13:6)

Destructive core belief: God doesn't care about me.
Opposite biblical core belief: I am precious in the sight of God and was created for a purpose.

God demonstrates his own love for us in this: While we
were still sinners, Christ died for us. (Romans 5:8).

I am convinced that neither death nor life, neither angels
nor demons, neither the present nor the future, nor any
powers, neither height nor depth, nor anything else in all
creation, will be able to separate us from the love of God
that is in Christ Jesus our Lord. (Romans 8:38–39)

Because of his great love for us, God, who is rich in mercy,
made us alive with Christ even when we were dead in
transgressions — it is by grace you have been saved. And
God raised us up with Christ and seated us with him in
the heavenly realms in Christ Jesus, in order that in the
coming ages he might show the incomparable riches of his
grace, expressed in his kindness to us in Christ Jesus. For it
is by grace you have been saved, through faith — and this
not from yourselves, it is the gift of God— not by works,
so that no one can boast. For we are God's workmanship,
created in Christ Jesus to do good works, which God
prepared in advance for us to do. (Ephesians 2:4–10)

Because we grow up in a world where sin is rampant, our core
beliefs are a mixed bag of destructive and biblical core beliefs.
Since it is the destructive core beliefs that cause problems, this
chapter focuses on those. Whenever you identify a destructive
core belief—a lie that Satan has implanted in you—there are several things you can do to replace it with a biblical core belief that
matches God's perspective of both you and the world.

- Create a simple statement that reflects biblical truth that
  you can use to replace the destructive core belief. Write this

on a card that you can look at from time to time. You can
see examples in the previous list of biblical core beliefs.

- Identify two or three Bible verses that are meaningful to
you that you can use to counter the destructive core belief.
If you are not yet familiar with the Bible, ask for help with
this from your pastor or a fellow believer who is mature in
Christ and knows the Bible well. Write the verses on a card
and post them where you can read them regularly until they
become a part of you. Use the previous examples as a model.
Keep in mind that there are many other verses that could
have been used. The key is to select verses that speak to you
personally and powerfully about the issue you're addressing.

- Whenever you notice that your thoughts, actions, or emotions are being driven by the destructive core belief, recall
the statement of truth you created and the verses that you
have memorized.

- Each day, ask God to help you eliminate this lie from your
life and replace it with His truth. Continue until you feel that
you are living the truth rather than the lie you identified.

- During your regular prayer time, think about the destructive core belief you identified as affecting your life. Have you
been able to effectively challenge it? If not ask God to help
you discern what you need to know or do to have victory in
this area of your life. If you have effectively challenged it,
praise God and thank Him for helping you with this.

- Ask someone you trust, who is strong in Christ, to be
an accountability partner. Having someone with whom
you can share your progress and setbacks is a time-tested
resource to strengthen your ability to change. Be sure to
ask this person to pray for you concerning the thoughts
and behaviors you are working to change. As James says,

"Confess your sins to each other and pray for each other so that you may be healed. The prayer of a righteous man is powerful and effective" (5:16).

THE NEED FOR SELF-EXAMINATION

It was mentioned earlier in the chapter that deep-seated core beliefs can contradict one's stated conscious beliefs. Sadly, people are often unaware of this difference. This is one reason both the Old and New Testament point out the value of taking time to look at your behavior and deciding whether it is consistent with what Scripture says. Here are several examples:

In your anger do not sin; when you are on your beds, search your hearts and be silent. (Psalm 4:4)

I have considered my ways and have turned my steps to your statutes. (Psalm 119:59)

Let us examine our ways and test them. (Lamentations 3:40)

Now this is what the Lord Almighty says: "Give careful thought to your ways." (Haggai 1:5)

A man ought to examine himself before he eats of the bread and drinks of the cup. (1 Corinthians 11:28)

Examine yourselves to see whether you are in the faith; test yourselves. Do you not realize that Christ Jesus is in you —unless, of course, you fail the test? (2 Corinthians 13:5)

Each one should test his own actions. Then he can take pride in himself, without comparing himself to somebody else. (Galatians 6:4)

Several factors can make it difficult to look at yourself honestly. People with negative self-images often avoid self-examination because they are filled with shame over their past and dread the increased shame that honest self-examination might bring. In contrast, people who take great pride in their superior abilities or accomplishments often avoid self-examination because it might make them aware of weaknesses or shortcomings that are difficult for them to admit. Sometimes, people avoid self-examination because of the tremendous emotional pain associated with areas of weakness.

In spite of the difficulty, honest self-examination is essential if you are to become the person God wants you to become. The good news is that you don't need to do this on your own. Invite God into the process and trust Him to reveal things to you at a pace you can handle and give you the strength and wisdom you need to overcome what you find.

One of the best opportunities for self-examination is during your daily prayer time. If your prayer time is in the morning, set aside a few minutes to look at your thoughts and behavior from the previous day. If your prayer time is in the evening, examine the day you've just completed. Identify the thoughts and behaviors that are in conflict with the teachings of Christ. As you do this, ask God to open your eyes and help you see what you need to change and to heal those areas of hurt from the past that need healing.

▶RECOMMENDED ACTIVITIES

TAKE AN INVENTORY OF YOUR BELIEFS

Go through the list of negative core beliefs, and place a check mark beside any that reflect either ideas that you've thought or said or feelings you've experienced about yourself or your circumstances.

Ask God to help you discern what you need to be aware of now that is hindering your spiritual life or keeping you from becoming the person He wants you to be. Then answer the following questions. As you answer them, keep in mind that they are intended to stimulate your thinking. Feel free to go beyond them and explore any other beliefs you might have that are associated with each area.

Beliefs about myself
- What are my strengths?
- What are my weaknesses?
- How would I describe my personality?
- How does God see me, both my strengths and areas where I need to mature and grow?
- Where am I most vulnerable to sin? What thoughts and actions are displeasing to God?

Beliefs about the nature of relationships
- How important are my relationships? Why?
- How should I interact with my co-workers, friends, family, and mate?
- How should I manage conflict?
- What should my friendships look like?
- What should I keep private?
- What parts of me are appropriate to share?
- Do I allow myself to be intimate with others? Why or why not?
- What would a truly intimate relationship look like? How would people interact?
- How do I act, think, and respond emotionally when I'm intimate with others?
- What qualities are required for intimacy? Which of these qualities do I have, and which do I need to work on?

Beliefs about the world

- How safe or dangerous is the world?
- How much control do I have over daily life?
- How well equipped am I to manage the problems I face in daily life?
- How well equipped am I to manage adversity such as the death of someone close to me, a financial set-back, or a major injury?

Beliefs about the nature of God

- Does God exist?
- How do I know this?
- What is He like? What are His characteristics and nature?
- Do I trust Him? How much?
- The Bible says that God is both just and gracious. How do I see these attributes actually manifesting in the world? In my life?
- How closely involved is God with my daily life?
- What should my relationship with God be like?

MAKE A LIST OF BEHAVIORS AND EMOTIONAL RESPONSES THAT DO NOT MATCH SCRIPTURE

Once you have completed the previous activity, set aside some time to examine your actions and emotional responses. Think about the various good and bad experiences you have had over the past few days. What did you do? How did you respond emotionally? What do your actions and emotional responses say about what you believe? List any that are in conflict with Scripture. Here are three examples of what people wrote as they did this exercise:

When I interact with people, I often act as if I believe that I have no value or am inferior to others. I also wrote that I should try to always be agreeable and compromise when people disagree with me. What I see is that I act as if I believe conflict is dangerous and I should avoid it at all costs.

I like to think of myself as being kind and compassionate. I can see many situations where I do act in this way. However, I also noticed that I like to point out weaknesses in others. While I usually do this in a humorous way that causes others to laugh, sometimes it makes the other person feel bad. I think my behavior and emotional reaction are saying that I think I'm better than others. Pointing out their shortcomings makes me feel superior.

I want to trust God. However, I notice that I worry a lot. Only rarely do my worries prove to be justified. I think I'm seeing that I don't really trust that God is in control and looking after me. I seem to act and feel like the world is a wild and dangerous place that can destroy me at any time.

CHANGING DESTRUCTIVE CORE BELIEFS

Once you've completed the previous activities, make a list of the destructive core beliefs you identified that you would like to change. Here are the destructive core beliefs that the people in each of the previous examples identified:

I have no value; conflict is dangerous.

I need to be number one and better than others.

The world is dangerous, and God is asleep at the wheel.

Once you have identified destructive core beliefs that you want to change, follow the guidelines that are detailed in this chapter and summarized below.

- Create a simple statement that reflects biblical truth.
- Identify two or three Bible verses that are meaningful to you that you can use to counter the destructive core belief.
- Whenever you notice that your thoughts, actions, or emotions are being driven by the destructive core belief, recall the statement of truth you created and the verses you have memorized.
- Each day, ask God to help you eliminate this lie from your life and to replace it with His truth.
- Reflect on progress and relapses into old behaviors during your regular prayer time.
- Find an accountability partner, and ask this person to pray regularly for you about this issue.

Be Grounded in God's Love

Guilt is what you feel when you've done something wrong. Shame is what you feel when you believe that you are bad or unacceptable in some way, either because of something you've done or because of something that's been done to you. Paul says that "godly sorrow brings repentance that leads to salvation and leaves no regret, but worldly sorrow brings death" (2 Corinthians 7:10). Godly sorrow is what you feel when you sin — when you act contrary to God's plan for your life, which both harms you and separates you from God. With real sin, you confess it and make restitution and the feelings of guilt and shame go away. Some people, however, experience tremendous shame and guilt that seems never to go away. This type of worldly sorrow is one of Satan's most effective tools for keeping a person in misery and separated from the power of God.

You may be struggling with feelings of guilt or shame or with the belief that you are worthless or unlovable. If so, it is essential that you stop and take some time to understand and connect with the forgiveness and love that are part of your relationship with God. Often, this is just too overwhelming of a task to do on your own. Find a pastor, a Christian counselor or a friend who you trust and who is mature in Christ to help you.

Here are several additional steps you can take now to begin to be freed from this type of false guilt and shame that produce worldly sorrow:

Understand What the Bible Says about Forgiveness and God's Love

- Read Romans 8:1–39.
- Memorize Romans 8:1 and John 3:16–17.
- Discuss these passages with a fellow Christian.

Pray for Deliverance from the Bondage that Shame and Guilt Have Produced

- Remember that "our struggle is not against flesh and blood, but against the rulers, against the authorities, against the powers of this dark world and against the spiritual forces of evil in the heavenly realms" (Ephesians 6:12).
- Ask others to pray for you about this.
- Here is an example of how to pray: "Father God, deliver me from the false guilt and shame that have held me prisoner for so long. Help me experience Your unconditional love, forgiveness, and affirmation at the very core of my being. When I sin, help me see it for what it is, human weakness that is common to all people. Then help me receive Your forgiveness for it and wherever possible set things right with those I have wronged. Help me be confident that this is all that You require. Help me know in the depths of my being that there is now no condemnation for those who are in

Christ Jesus because through Christ Jesus the law of the
Spirit of life has set me free from the law of sin and death.
Fill me with Your Holy Spirit and empower me to see
both myself and the world as You see them and live as You
would have me live. Thank you, Father, for hearing and
answering my prayer. In Jesus' precious name, amen."

Challenge Worldly Sorrow

- When you experience feelings of guilt or shame, identify
  whether it is due to a real sin you have committed recently
  or due to something in your past.
- If your guilt and shame are due to real sin, ask God for forgiveness and decide what you can do, if anything, to make
  amends for what you've done. Here is a simple model of
  how to approach someone you've wronged:
  - Repent: "I'm sorry for what I did."
  - Ask for forgiveness: "Please forgive me."
  - Ask to make amends: "Is there anything I can do to
    make up for it?" (You may already know what you should
    do. If so, ask them, "May I. . . ")
- If your guilt and shame are due to something in your past,
  recall the verses you memorized and ask God to help you
  know and feel the truth.

CHAPTER 7

THE WINDOW OF
THE SOUL

The Gospels describe how a young man approached Jesus and asked "What must I do to inherit eternal life?" (Mark 10:17 and Luke 18:18) After the young man declared that he had kept all the commandments since he was a boy, "Jesus looked at him and loved him. 'One thing you lack,' he said. 'Go, sell everything you have and give to the poor, and you will have treasure in heaven. Then come, follow me.' At this the man's face fell. He went away sad, because he had great wealth" (Mark 10:21–22).

This story is not about needing to become poor in order to be a Christian, but about determining what is most important to you. Jesus looked into this young man's soul and challenged him on an issue where the man's own emotional response revealed his true priorities more powerfully than words could ever express. In the same way, your emotional reactions to everyday events reveal what is most important to you and what you believe in the depths of your soul. Truly, emotions are the window of the soul. You just need to pay attention.

In this chapter we begin our exploration of the spiritual side of your emotions as a window into your soul. But first, I would like to explore a subject that is uncomfortable for many: our limited knowledge about God and the spiritual world.

BECOME COMFORTABLE WITH NOT KNOWING

There are many aspects of reality about which the Bible is either silent or very vague. For example, Genesis begins with the statement, "In the beginning God created the heavens and the earth" (Genesis 1:1). It tells us nothing about what was going on before this happened or why God chose to act when and how He did. It simply declares that God is the Creator of everything we see.

In a similar way, the Bible describes various aspects of the spiritual realm but often leaves out many of the details. For example, we know that there are angels, demons, and a spirit being who opposes God, seeking to frustrate His plans, and lead His people into rebellion. Many different names are used for this being such as Satan, the devil, and Lucifer. We know that Satan will be defeated, but we do not know exactly when. We know that when we are in Christ, we become part of God's plan for defeating Satan and restoring creation to what it is meant to be, but we do not know all the details of how God is using us. While we would like to know more, the Bible gives us enough of a glimpse into the spiritual realm to alert us to important spiritual blessings and dangers.

The Bible's main focus is on the here and now. Much is said about how we can have a rich relationship with God and how we should treat others. There is also a wealth of detail about how one can experience blessings and live a truly fulfilling life. The problem is that, like Adam and Eve, we want to "be like God" and know everything He knows. In addition, we want to be in control of our lives and all the situations we encounter.

At some point, we need to accept that a limited physical person cannot understand an unlimited and omnipotent God who exists outside of time and space as we know it. We also need to accept that there are many aspects of our lives that we cannot control and trust that God has a plan for our lives that is far better than anything we could come up with. This is the essence of what it means to "live by faith, not by sight" (2 Corinthians 5:7).

One way to gain understanding of what it means to live by faith is to look at the relationship between children and loving parents. Because children have limited experience and knowledge there are many times when they want to do things that would be harmful or keep them from developing in a healthy way. Because parents have knowledge and experience that allows them to see the big picture, they understand what is good and bad for children. Unfortunately, the immaturity of children often prevents them from understanding what it is that a parent is explaining to them. The wise child simply trusts that the parent knows best. This is the essence of faith: believing that God knows us better than we know ourselves, truly wants what is best for us, and knows better than we do what we should be doing and not doing to obtain it.

Unfortunately, we are often unwise children in regard to our heavenly Father. Instead of trusting that He knows what we need even before we ask (Matthew 6:8), we complain and resist His leading. One of the most difficult aspects of faith is accepting how truly incompetent we are when it comes to managing our lives. This tendency to mismanage our lives when left to our own resources is due to two things: our sinful nature and the fact that our knowledge will always be limited and incomplete—we simply do not have the capacity to understand the physical and spiritual world we live in as thoroughly as God does.

That is why the Bible only gives us a limited view of the spiritual world. When a concept is too difficult for children to understand or might cause them to grow inquisitive about matters that would prove harmful, the wise parent provides a simple explanation. In the same way, God, through the Bible, has given us as much information as we need and can understand along with all the directions we need to live the life we are meant to live.

WHAT DOES "SPIRITUAL" MEAN?

Before we can adequately explore the spiritual side of emotions, we need to define what we mean when we use the word *spiritual*. In psychology and philosophy, the term *spiritual* usually refers to what are often called existential beliefs. These include the various beliefs one has about the meaning of existence: "What's the purpose of life?" "How does one achieve happiness?" and so on. These types of "spiritual" issues are really just a part of your belief system and, as such, a part of the mental aspect of emotions discussed in chapters 5 and 6. We pointed out in those chapters that your beliefs about the nature of the world and the meaning of life do play a key role in how you interpret events, which in turn affects the various emotional responses you have.

From a biblical perspective, however, a person's spiritual nature means something quite different than from a psychological or philosophical perspective. When the Bible speaks of your spiritual side, it is referring to a real but immaterial part of yourself. The two words that are most often used to describe the spiritual aspect of your being are *soul* and *spirit*. Unfortunately, these words are used in so many different ways, that the exact nature of your spirit and soul remain something of a mystery.

Your Soul and Spirit

In the Old Testament the Hebrew word *nephesh* is the word that is usually translated as "soul." The corresponding Greek word in the New Testament is *psuche*. The most basic meaning of these words is simply "life" as in Exodus 21:23, "If there is serious injury, you are to take life for life [Hebrew: *nephesh*]," or John 15:13, "Greater love has no one than this, that he lay down his life [Greek: *psuche*] for his friends." In addition to being used as a synonym for life, the soul is also described as the source or center of many spiritual and emotional experiences as well the immaterial side of humans. Here are a few examples:

> Why are you downcast, O my soul? Why so disturbed within me? (Psalm 43:5)

> Surely my soul remembers and is bowed down within me. (Lamentations 3:20, NASB)

> Then my soul will rejoice in the Lord and delight in his salvation. (Psalm 35:9)

> My [God's] soul has no pleasure in him. (Hebrews 10:38, NASB)

> Then [Jesus] said to them, "My soul is overwhelmed with sorrow . . . " (Matthew 26:38)

Now My soul has become troubled; and what shall I say . . . ? (John 12:27, NASB)

Obey them not only to win their favor when their eye is on you, but like slaves of Christ, doing the will of God from your heart (Ephesians 6:6; in the Greek: "from your soul").

Attempts to define what the Bible means by *spirit* generate the same level of confusion as attempts to define what is meant by *soul*. In the Old Testament the Hebrew word *ruach* is used for "spirit." In the New Testament it is the Greek word *pneuma*. Again, both these words are used in a wide variety of ways. While they are often used to speak of the immaterial part of man, they are also used in many other contexts. Here are just a few examples:

His back has rows of shields tightly sealed together; each is so close to the next that no air [Hebrew: ruach] can pass between. (Job 41:15–16)

[God] forms the spirit of man within him . . . (Zechariah 12:1)

The dust returns to the ground it came from, and the spirit returns to God who gave it. (Ecclesiastes 12:7)

The wind [Greek: pneuma] blows wherever it pleases. You hear its sound, but you cannot tell where it comes from or where it is going. So it is with everyone born of the Spirit [Greek: pneuma]. (John 3:8)

The Spirit himself testifies with our spirit . . . (Romans 8:16)

Her spirit returned, and at once she stood up. Then Jesus told them to give her something to eat. (Luke 8:55)

To confuse things even more, the words *soul* and *spirit* are sometimes used in parallel in Hebrew poetry and, thus, are being used as synonyms. Here is both an Old Testament and a New Testament example of this:

My soul yearns for you in the night; in the morning my spirit longs for you. (Isaiah 26:9)

Mary said: My soul exalts the Lord, and my spirit has rejoiced in God my Savior. (Luke 1:46–47, NASB)

Because spirit and soul are used in so many different and overlapping ways, there is no agreement among theologians and biblical scholars as to the exact nature of your soul and spirit. However, most adopt one of two general viewpoints: a two-part view of human nature or a three-part view. It is important to emphasize that both perspectives see these parts as simply different aspects of a single unity.

The first viewpoint sees humans as having two basic parts: material and immaterial, physical and non-physical. Karl Barth, the well-known theologian, states that a person is "bodily soul, as he is also besouled body." In this perspective, a person cannot exist in just a body nor can a person be a bodiless spirit, except in a temporary, transitional state. Another way to say this is "You are a soul that has both a body and a spirit."

The second viewpoint sees humans has having a three-part nature: body, soul, and spirit. In this perspective, each has a different function: the body, world-consciousness; the soul, self-consciousness; and the spirit, God-consciousness. Two verses are cited to support this position:

> May God himself, the God of peace, sanctify you through and through. May your whole spirit, soul and body be kept blameless at the coming of our Lord Jesus Christ. (1 Thessalonians 5:23)

> The word of God is living and active. Sharper than any double-edged sword, it penetrates even to dividing soul and spirit, joints and marrow; it judges the thoughts and attitudes of the heart. (Hebrews 4:12)

In light of this uncertainty and disagreement among mainstream people of faith, who have spent their lives studying the Scriptures, the following perspective is used in this book: *Your spirit is that aspect of your immaterial part that interacts with the spiritual dimension of creation.* It is also the part of you that is regenerated when you accept Christ and which becomes united with the Holy Spirit. This is what Paul is referring to when he says, "He who unites himself with the Lord is one with him in spirit" (1 Corinthians 6:17). Here the word *Lord* is referring to the Holy Spirit. Thus, Paul is saying that union with the Lord is a union of the human spirit with His Spirit, the Holy Spirit. Here are a few more verses that reflect this idea:

> Jesus answered, "Truly, truly, I say to you, unless one is born of water and the Spirit he cannot enter into the kingdom of God. That which is born of the flesh is flesh, and that which is born of the Spirit is spirit." (John 3:5–6, NASB)

> Father, just as you are in me and I am in you. May they also be in us. (John 17:21)

> If anyone is in Christ, he is a new creation; the old has gone, the new has come! (2 Corinthians 5:16–17)

If anyone acknowledges that Jesus is the Son of God, God lives in him and he in God. (1 John 4:15)

In order to understand how the joining of our spirit with the Holy Spirit affects our emotions, we need to first take a quick look at what it means to be separated from God's Spirit.

SEPARATION FROM GOD

In the first chapter of Genesis we see that people were meant to be the crown of God's creation. We were made in His image and given stewardship of the earth. In the second chapter we see that we were meant to live in harmonious relationship with Him and one another. In the third chapter we see how this harmonious relationship was broken causing sin and corruption to enter the world when Adam and Eve sought to "be like God, knowing good and evil" (Genesis 3:5). When Adam and Eve made this choice, their spirit became separated from God's Spirit.

This separation from God, along with the desire to make ourselves god by living life according to our own rules instead of following God, has been passed on to every generation since theirs. This is why Christ came to earth in flesh and sacrificed Himself on our behalf. Joining with Him restores our relationship to what it was meant to be. This in turn allows the Holy Spirit to begin a process called sanctification in which our character slowly begins to become more and more like that of Christ—a process that is never fully completed in this life.

When you are separated from God, you do not have direct access to God's wisdom and power. For the most part, your emotions are generated and controlled by your mind and body as described in the previous chapters. This is why Paul says, "The flesh sets its desire against the Spirit, and the Spirit against the flesh; for these are in opposition to one another" (Galatians 5:17). However, separation from God also means that your spirit becomes open to those realms of the spiritual dimension opposed to God: the devil and his legions. Indeed, even though the influence of Satan will eventually be eliminated, for now, he is referred to as "the god of this age" who "has blinded the minds of unbelievers" (2 Corinthians 4:4). For some mysterious reason he has been given authority over the earth at this time. We know this because he offered worldly power to Jesus as one of his temptations when he said, "I will give you all their authority and splendor, for it has been given to me, and I can give it to anyone I want to" (Luke 4:6).

The good news is that when you are joined to Christ, "the one who is in you is greater than the one who is in the world" (1 John 4:4). You now have access to wisdom and power beyond what you had when you were walking "according to the flesh" (Romans 8:4, NASB). Indeed, "The Spirit searches all things, even the deep things of God. For who among men knows the thoughts of a man except the man's spirit within him? In the same way no one knows the thoughts of God except the Spirit of God. We have not received the spirit of the world but the Spirit who is from God, that we may understand what God has freely given us" (1 Corinthians 2:10-12).

In the following chapters we will come back to this idea and how the key to accessing this wisdom and power is to walk "according to the Spirit" (Romans 8:4, NASB).

HOW EMOTIONS REVEAL YOUR TRUE SPIRITUAL CONDITION

It has been said that adversity reveals our true character. Adversity also reveals the true character of our faith and the nature of our relationship with God. It is when we undergo periods of trial that we see who we really are and can experience many of the deeper aspects of God's love and care. Emotions play a key role in this process. By simply watching your emotional reactions to the various events that occur in your life, you can see where spiritual growth has taken place as well as where immaturity still exists.

Jerry and Kathy, the couple whose story opened this book, offer a good example of how emotions reveal your spiritual character. Those who knew Kathy and Jerry thought of them as mature Christians. However, the struggle they went through as a result of the death of their babies revealed some of their unbiblical beliefs about God. The struggle also revealed areas of their life where they still didn't fully trust God.

One idea that Kathy and Jerry struggled with was the belief that if we are faithful, we will be blessed. This is often misunderstood as meaning, "If I'm faithful, I will not suffer from hardships." While God does bless us abundantly when we are faithful, we are not exempt from suffering. To see this, one need only look at the examples of how saints such as Paul and others in the early church suffered. We live in a broken world where even our genetic make-up has been tainted by sin. That is why Jesus said, "I have told you these things, so that in me you may have peace. In this world you will have trouble. But take heart! I have overcome the world" (John 16:33). As Jerry and Kathy worked through their grief and anger towards God, they came to understand how God blesses us in new and deeper ways each day.

Another area they struggled with was the desire that we all share to tell God how to run our lives rather than allowing Him to be in control. Kathy and Jerry had their hearts and minds set on two healthy babies who would be model children and become ardent followers of Christ. There is nothing wrong with wanting this. However, what they experienced was the agony of two still-born children. This was definitely not what they had planned and they struggled with the question, "How can you trust a God who allows this to happen?"

Over time, they learned through the suffering they experienced that God is not the author of evil. Rather, He can and does transform the evil that results from our brokenness and living in a broken world that is under the influence of Satan into what is good for those who truly trust and depend on Him. The ministry that Kathy and Jerry developed working with parents in pain is only one example of this.

▶Recommended Activities

Reflect on What Your Emotions Reveal about Your Spiritual Character

In the Recommended Activities for previous chapters you were asked to begin recording examples of times when you experienced strong emotions and make a list of behaviors and emotional responses that are contrary to what Scripture teaches. Use one or two of the examples that you recorded for this exercise. If you did not do these exercises, take some time this week to reflect on the previous two or three days. Identify times when you were experiencing negative emotions such as anxiety, fear, anger, disappointment, or depression. Give a brief description of each event along with any thoughts you had and the emotions you were experiencing.

You are now ready to see what God has to teach you. Begin by asking God to reveal to you those broken areas of your life that you need to see in this situation and to help you accept what He is showing you. Now, select the experience that provoked the strongest emotion, and answer the following questions:

- Did my behavior damage a relationship or cause harm to myself or someone else? If so, how?
- Was I acting or thinking in a way that is contrary to principles taught in the Bible? If so, which ones?
- What did my thoughts, emotions, and actions reveal about my true beliefs?
  - What was the most important consideration for me right then?
  - What was my main fear or desire at that moment?
  - What would be a simple statement of the thought or rule that was guiding my behavior at the time? (See chapter 6 for examples.)
- What does my emotional reaction to this event at that time reveal about my spiritual character?
  - Did I have any thoughts about God at this time?
  - How did I view God when I reflected on this event—as a loving father, an unfair tyrant, or something else?
  - Was I trusting God and leaning on His strength or only on my own abilities? Why?
  - What does this say about my relationship with God?
- What is the lesson I need to learn from this experience?
- What specifically do I need to ask for in prayer so I may learn this lesson?
- What Bible verse or passage would help me with this issue?
- What do I need to do? (Be very specific as to action, time, and place.)

Be sure to write out your answers and then spend some time reviewing what you have written during your prayer and meditation time. Record any insights that come to you during your time in prayer. Here is an example written by Kim, a quiet, shy lady who is struggling to learn how to stand up for herself.

Description of the event:
Last Thursday I was having lunch with one of my friends. I wanted a taco salad but my friend said, "That's no good, get the Asian salad instead." I felt shame and embarrassment and quickly said, "Oh I didn't know that" and ordered the Asian salad even though I actually wanted the taco salad. Later, when I was alone, I became very angry. I was thinking, "Who does she think she is telling me what to order? I never want to see her again!"

Analysis
Did my behavior damage a relationship or cause harm to myself or someone else? If so, how?
The only one who was harmed was myself. I should have just said, "No, I've had the taco salad before and I really like it." Doing that would not have harmed anyone and is what any confident adult would have done. When I don't stand up for myself, I'm the one who walks away feeling embarrassed, angry, and resentful. This damaged the relationship because I put up a wall and did not want to say anything to her after this happened.

Was I acting or thinking in a way that is contrary to principles taught in the Bible? If so, which ones?
I was filled with bitterness and anger and thinking hateful thoughts about my friend. This is not what God wants. All of this happened because I was not "speaking the truth in love" as it says in Ephesians 4:15. While my actions need to be loving, they also need to be honest. When I don't speak the truth because it might make someone not like me, I'm actually

lying. The Bible says to "let your 'Yes' be 'Yes,' and your 'No,' 'No'" (Matthew 5:37). This means I need to be honest when I speak. I know that instead of always trying to please others I should strive to please God.

What did my thoughts, emotions, and actions reveal about my true beliefs?
The main thing that I see in this situation is that I desperately want the approval of others and will do anything to avoid conflict. I act as if I believe that I must always keep the peace and never do anything that might upset someone.

What does my emotional reaction to this event reveal about my spiritual character?
I feel very weak and insignificant. I often think that when God looks at me He must be very disappointed. I've sometimes thought that God must think that He made a mistake when He made me or that maybe there's no way that He can love me. I know in my head that these things are not true, but I struggle with knowing them in my heart.

I tend to see God as being like my parents who were very strict and very critical. Sometimes, I'm afraid of God.

What is the lesson I need to learn from this experience?
The lesson is one that I've been aware of for some time. I need to learn to trust my own judgment and believe that God made me the way I'm supposed to be. I also need to take actions based on that judgment instead of letting others always tell me what I should do and stop worrying so much about what other people think and be honest when speaking my mind. I can do this in a kind way. I also need to separate God from my parents and see Him as He really is.

What specifically do I need to ask for in prayer in order to learn this lesson?
I think I need two things. First, I need confidence. Second, I think I need to ask God to help me really understand and experience more deeply how much I'm loved by Him. The coldness and critical nature of my parents made me think that there was something wrong and unlovable about me. This lie has crippled me all of my life. God is not like my parents!

What Bible verse or passage would help me with this issue?
Two Bible verses that can remind me to speak up with confidence are 2 Timothy 1:7: "For God did not give us a spirit of timidity, but a spirit of power, of love and of self-discipline," and Matthew 5:37: "Let your 'Yes' be 'Yes,' and your 'No,' 'No.'"

The verses that speak the most clearly to me about God's love are John 3:16–17: "For God so loved the world that he gave his one and only Son, that whoever believes in him shall not perish but have eternal life. For God did not send his Son into the world to condemn the world, but to save the world through him," and Matthew 11:29: "Take my yoke upon you and learn from me, for I am gentle and humble in heart, and you will find rest for your souls."

What do I need to do?
During my prayer time, I need to take some time to think about the verses I've chosen and ask God to give me the strength and wisdom I need each day to say what I think and feel in a loving but honest and assertive way.

When I've talked about this with Mary, she has suggested that I might want to join the women's group at church so I can experience true Christian love. I think this would help me, but I've always been too scared to do this. I need God to give me the strength to join our women's group and then attend so I can form some healthy relationships and practice expressing myself with people who are safe.

CHAPTER 8

EMOTIONS AND GOD'S WILL FOR YOU

Throughout history, people have asked, "Why am I here?" As discussed in chapters 5 and 6, our answer to this question becomes the basis of many of the core beliefs that drive our thoughts, actions, and emotions. Yet, while we've explored many ways in which emotions serve us, our understanding of emotions is incomplete until we look more closely at this life-shaping question. In doing so we glimpse some of the majesty of how God uses emotions to fit us into His plans.

WHY IS UNDERSTANDING MY PURPOSE IMPORTANT?

It is impossible to have a full understanding of a man-made machine if you do not understand the purpose for which it was made. Once you understand why it was invented, the various parts make sense in a way that is very different from simply understanding how it was put together and how the various parts work.

To illustrate this, consider the example of a claw hammer found by a person who has never seen or heard of hammers or nails. It would be easy for this person to see how the hammer was constructed. It's just a finished piece of wood attached to an odd shaped piece of metal. While this person may not know the true purpose for the hammer, many other uses might be found for it: to open nuts, to pound on things, or maybe even to use as a weapon. However, the true reason it was created—to drive and remove nails—would be a complete mystery.

This person would probably be at an even greater loss to explain the "claw" part of the hammer that is used to remove nails. Maybe it's a decoration or something with ritualistic significance. Perhaps it's a back-scratcher! It is only when one learns about nails and how the hammer was designed to drive and remove them from wood that its design and use become clear. In the same way, the purpose of emotions can only be fully grasped when viewed within the context of why God created us.

Physics looks at the universe as a complex system of matter and energy governed by a set of laws but interacting randomly. Thus, all of creation, including humans, has no specific purpose. It just "happened" as a result of random events. Biology refines this a little and views organisms within the perspective of the theory of evolution and natural selection. Since species only survive by reproducing themselves, the function of emotions, like all our other functions is to help the various species survive, reproduce, and perpetuate themselves. Psychology takes this same view. As discussed in previous chapters, psychology has identified several ways in which emotions do help us survive by organizing information in terms of importance, alerting us to important events and things in our environment, and aiding in communication.

In contrast, the Bible's view of the universe sees both a Creator and an overarching order and plan that go beyond the basic functions identified by science. One of the key features of the biblical view of the universe is a clearly defined purpose for our lives. When theologians speak about this purpose, they usually do it in the context of what is known as God's will which is usually seen as having three different aspects: God's sovereign will, God's moral will, and God's individual will.

THREE ASPECTS OF GOD'S WILL

God's sovereign will refers to the fact that God is sovereign and His will can never be frustrated. This is also called God's decretive will or efficacious will since God decrees what happens and His will is always effective in bringing about what He wants. Another aspect of God's sovereign will is His sovereign plan or ultimate will. This refers to His predetermined plan for creation that He ordained from the beginning of time.

As discussed in chapter 7, God's plan for creation was to have people, the crown of His creation, live in harmonious relationship with him, each other, and creation itself. This is obviously not the case in our world, so theologians also speak of God's permissive will in conjunction with God's sovereign will. God allows both humans and angels to make moral choices that are contrary to His sovereign plan. He also allows the consequences of those choices whether they are good or evil. As a result, God's sovereign plan can also be described as His hidden will, since many of the details about how God is working to bring about His sovereign plan cannot be known by us at this time.

A second aspect of God's will is His moral will. God's moral will is also referred to as His preceptive will since it describes the precepts or principles that we are to live by. These are the things that are pleasing to God as described in the Law and demonstrated in the life of Christ. Since this aspect of God's will is also a reflection of His character or disposition, God's moral will is also referred to as His will of disposition.

Finally, one can speak of God's individual will which is also referred to as God's specific will or ideal will. God's individual will is what Christians are most commonly speaking of when they talk about God's will. God's individual will is also the aspect of God's will that is most often misunderstood.

Many Christians believe that God has an ideal, detailed life-plan uniquely designed for each person. People with this view then believe that it is their responsibility to find that perfect place where they are supposed to be—that one mate, one job, one ministry, etc.—if they are going to be "in the center of God's will". They often further believe that if they fail to discover these details, they miss out on what was meant for them. Here are two examples of Old Testament Scriptures used to support this type of thinking:

> Trust in the LORD with all your heart and lean not on your own understanding; in all your ways acknowledge him, and he will make your paths straight. (Proverbs 3:5–6)

> I will instruct you and teach you in the way you should go; I will counsel you and watch over you. (Psalm 32:8)

When you look at these verses in context, you realize that *path* and *way* do not refer to every aspect of your life, but to your general course of life when lived according to God's moral will. The same mistake is made with New Testament verses used to support this view. One example:

> Be very careful, then, how you live—not as unwise but as wise, making the most of every opportunity, because the days are evil. Therefore do not be foolish, but understand what the Lord's will is. (Ephesians 5:15–17)

Again, when read in context, the phrase *understand what the Lord's will is* refers to understanding God's moral will, the godly way in which we are to live, not to specific details.

The truth is that God's individual will for you is not a hidden secret that you have to seek out. God does not hide Himself or what He wants from you. In fact, the Bible is very clear that we are able to know God's will. Paul, while discussing God's moral will admonishes us to "not be foolish, but understand what the Lord's will is" (Ephesians 5:17). In Romans, while discussing our need to conform to God's moral will, he boldly states that "you will be able to test and approve what God's will is" (12:2). Jesus himself said, "If anyone chooses to do God's will, he will find out whether my teaching comes from God or whether I speak on my own" (John 7:17).

It turns out that what God wants is the same for every believer. It is not a specific rigid plan, but rather a *goal*: "to be conformed to the likeness of his Son" (Romans 8:29). One of the most amazing parts of God's plan for your life is the freedom that you have as you yield your life to Him and allow Him to move you towards this goal.

Jesus said, "If you hold to my teaching, you are really my disciples. Then you will know the truth, and the truth will set you free" (John 8:31–32). A few verses later he says, "So if the Son sets you free, you will be free indeed" (verse 36). When we look at Scripture, we see that this freedom is not just freedom from sin, but includes freedom from the tyranny of desires, legalism, and the many lies of this world. With this freedom comes many good things that we are free to choose from with only one limit: we are to live within God's moral will.

The Problem with Looking at God's Individual Will as a Specific, Detailed Plan

The Bible provides principles for living life in a way that is pleasing to God. It does not tell you the name of the person you should marry or the exact place where you should live. This creates a problem for people who believe that God's individual will is a detailed and precise plan for every aspect of your life: How do you discover these details?

While God does sometimes talk directly to a person in an audible voice or send an angelic messenger, these are unusual occurrences. How, then, can those who believe this way discover the details of God's plan for their lives so they can be in the "center of God's will?" The answer is that they often use emotions or "impressions" to determine God's specific will in a situation.

Those who believe that one needs a strong subjective experience to know what God wants sometimes come to see themselves as being unworthy or abandoned by God when they don't experience these feelings. Those who claim to have had this type of experience and to know God's will often feel that they have special knowledge of God that sets them apart from others. Sometimes, when people with this belief fail to have this type of subjective experience, they give up and abandon their faith. Sadly, in seeking specific details in this way, most usually miss the joy and richness of God's plan for their lives.

GOD'S MORAL WILL *IS* HIS INDIVIDUAL WILL FOR YOU

God's individual will for you is usually more concerned with the big picture—your heart, character, and the moral choices you make—than the small details of life. Yes, God often will have a specific assignment for you. He might bring a hurting soul into your life or point you to a ministry that He wants you to pursue. Sometimes He even prompts specific words, thoughts, or actions that allow you to be His instrument in a specific situation. However, He leaves most of the details of how to help someone or work in your ministry up to you.

One of the wonders of how God works in our lives is the way He allows us the freedom to make choices. He then works with these choices to both build our character and carry out His plans for creation. Unfortunately, many people don't understand this. In fact, many view God's moral will as a restriction that keeps them from enjoying the really good things in life. This is unfortunate because conforming to God's moral will actually enables us to experience the best that life has to offer.

While recounting the law to the Jews, Moses put it this way: "This day I call heaven and earth as witnesses against you that I have set before you life and death, blessings and curses. Now choose life, so that you and your children may live" (Deuteronomy 30:19). God wants us to choose a rich life full of love and a dynamic relationship with Him. Unfortunately, our sin nature—the desire to be our own god and call the shots—often causes us to make choices that lead us away from God.

An often used analogy compares God's moral will to traffic laws. If I want to go from my home in Sacramento, California to New York City, I am free to take any one of a thousand different routes. As I travel to New York, I could choose to take my time and make frequent stops. I could even choose to take side trips and enjoy a particular spot for several days. If I wanted, I could choose to get there as fast as possible, stopping only to eat and sleep.

On each road there would be many signs to help me know where I am and the direction I need to take to get to where I am going. These are like the many examples and principles in the Bible that clearly explain how to deal with most of the situations I encounter in life. All I need to do to reach New York safe and sound is to read the signs and obey the laws that allow drivers to share the roads safely.

If I don't pay attention to the signs, I'll probably end up going the wrong way and far from my destination. If I drive too fast or carelessly, I'll receive traffic tickets for minor violations and might even be thrown in jail for a major violation—the natural penalty of sin. Even worse, if I choose to drive recklessly, I might harm or kill myself and others.

Now regardless of the route I choose, it is possible that I will encounter roadwork or some type of danger, such as a bridge that has been washed out. At these locations there will probably be someone in the middle of the road telling me to take an alternate route. In the same way, God does sometimes give you a very personal and specific communication about a danger you are facing or something He wants you to do. However, most of the time, you are free to make your own decisions. The only limitation is that you give your best effort to make decisions that conform to God's moral will. To help us with this, God has provided us with the Bible, the Holy Spirit, pastors, and fellow Christians. Returning to the example of an imaginary road trip, it's like having a friend in the seat next to you with a map noting signs that point you in the right direction and alerting you to danger.

What then is God's moral will? It is living a life that reflects God's character as described in the law and the life of Jesus. Here is a small sample of the many verses that make this clear:

> Jesus replied: "'Love the Lord your God with all your heart and with all your soul and with all your mind.' This is the first and greatest commandment. And the second is like it: 'Love your neighbor as yourself.' All the Law and the Prophets hang on these two commandments." (Matthew 22:37–40)

> Let your light shine before men, that they may see your good deeds and praise your Father in heaven. (Matthew 5:16)

> Whoever does God's will is my brother and sister and mother. (Mark 3:35)

> He replied, "My mother and brothers are those who hear God's word and put it into practice." (Luke 8:21)

> If you love me, you will obey what I command. (John 14:15)

> If you remain in me and my words remain in you, ask whatever you wish, and it will be given you. This is to my Father's glory, that you bear much fruit, showing yourselves to be my disciples. (John 15:7–8)

> So whether you eat or drink or whatever you do, do it all for the glory of God. (1 Corinthians 10:31)

> We are God's workmanship, created in Christ Jesus to do good works, which God prepared in advance for us to do. (Ephesians 2:10)

His intent was that now, through the church, the manifold wisdom of God should be made known to the rulers and authorities in the heavenly realms, according to his eternal purpose which he accomplished in Christ Jesus our Lord. (Ephesians 3:10–11)

Be imitators of God, therefore, as dearly loved children and live a life of love, just as Christ loved us and gave himself up for us as a fragrant offering and sacrifice to God. (Ephesians 5:1–2)

God did not call us to be impure, but to live a holy life. Therefore, he who rejects this instruction does not reject man but God, who gives you his Holy Spirit. (1 Thessalonians 4:7–8)

Be joyful always; pray continually; give thanks in all circumstances, for this is God's will for you in Christ Jesus. (1 Thessalonians 5:12–18)

Be holy, because I am holy. (1 Peter 1:15–16)

Live such good lives among the pagans that, though they accuse you of doing wrong, they may see your good deeds and glorify God on the day he visits us. (1 Peter 2:12)

The Old Testament is very clear about the types of actions and thoughts that are pleasing to God and conform to His moral will. It also clearly shows that it is impossible for us to conform to God's will on our own. Even when I understand God's word, my spirit and nature cause me to think and act in ways that are contrary to God's will. But as the New Testament reveals, the restoration of my relationship with God through Christ opens the door for the Holy Spirit to cleanse my mind and spirit so that, more and more, conforming to God's will is not an act of human will but a natural part of my renewed nature and Christ living in me.

How Emotions Fit into God's Plan

In chapter 2 you learned about the subjective, experiential side of emotions and how discussions on emotions often overlook this aspect of them. This is also one of the often overlooked purposes of emotions: to *experience* the love of God. John clearly states, "God is love" (1 John 4:8, 16). Since we are created in the image of God, I believe that one of the chief purposes of emotions is to allow us to experience that love, both in our relationship with God and with one another. Indeed, the imagery of lovers is used throughout the Bible to describe the type of relationship God wants us to have with Him.

In addition, the Old Testament frequently tells how God was "pleased" with various people. For example, He told Moses, "I am pleased with you" (Exodus 33:17). In Hebrews we read that Enoch, "was commended as one who pleased God" (11:5). We also read in many places that God "delights" in His people. Here are a few examples:

> The Lord be exalted, who delights in the well-being of his servant. (Psalm 35:27)

> For the Lord takes delight in his people; he crowns the humble with salvation. (Psalm 149:4)

> The Lord detests men of perverse heart, but he delights in those whose ways are blameless. (Proverbs 11:20)

It is no wonder then that love, joy, and peace are the first fruits of the Spirit mentioned by Paul in Galatians 5:22.

We see then, that one of the purposes of emotions is to share in the experience of love and joy that are the essence of God. James declares: "Every good and perfect gift is from above, coming down from the Father of the heavenly lights, who does not change like shifting shadows" (1:17). No greater gift can be imagined than the gift of being able to experience the intimacy that God offers.

This ability to experience intimacy with God is perhaps one of the most awesome aspects of emotions, but it's not the whole story. In previous chapters, we've seen how emotions move us to take action and help us respond to danger, learn and prioritize information, and communicate with one another. Each of these functions of emotions has a spiritual side that, when functioning under the direction of the Holy Spirit, can alert us to spiritual dangers, enable us to understand God's nature and will, and help us listen and respond to God's leading.

Chapter 5 discusses in detail how most of your emotions are the result of the interpretations you make of events. I firmly believe that if I truly saw the world the way God sees it, then my emotions would always be in line with God's will. I would rejoice in the things that please God and hate only those things that are detestable to Him. Unfortunately, I live in a body and world tainted by sin. I have beliefs that are still influenced by the world and contrary to the way God thinks. I also have an array of automatic emotional responses that were developed while I was fully under the influence of the brokenness of the world.

When those aspects of my life that are still infected with Satan's lies, sin, or worldly conditioning are influencing my thinking and my emotions, it causes me to act in ways that I know are not pleasing to God. Paul put it this way: "I have the desire to do what is good, but I cannot carry it out. For what I do is not the good I want to do; no, the evil I do not want to do—this I keep on doing" (Romans 7:18–19). But this is not the end of the story.

I also cry out with Paul, "What a wretched man I am! Who will rescue me from this body of death? Thanks be to God—through Jesus Christ our Lord!" (Romans 7:24–25).

Because I belong to Jesus, I know that "in all things God works for the good of those who love him, who have been called according to his purpose" (Romans 8:28). I can also say with Paul that "I am convinced that neither death nor life, neither angels nor demons, neither the present nor the future, nor any powers, neither height nor depth, nor anything else in all creation, will be able to separate us from the love of God that is in Christ Jesus our Lord" (Romans 8:38–39).

As God's Word refreshes and renews my mind, His Spirit also refreshes and renews my spirit so that I can more clearly hear God and see events through God's eyes. This, in turn, allows my emotions to work increasingly as God intended them to work. I want to emphasize that this is not a purely mental process. Renewing the mind is important. However, our union with God through Christ in some mysterious way allows us to experience God's reactions to events within our own being. At first this is just a fleeting feeling that we can easily ignore if we choose. As we draw nearer to God, it becomes so overwhelming that it cannot be ignored.

As God looks through me, I become saddened by hard hearts, rejoice with souls won, am moved to act against injustice, find patience when the brokenness of others rubs me the wrong way, and love in an ever deepening manner. But this is a slow process. All too often my thoughts, actions, and emotions are still in conflict with His Word and stifle the flow of His Spirit through me. Each time this happens it provides me with an opportunity to discover yet another way that my life needs to be restored. Indeed, Jesus promised that "the Counselor, the Holy Spirit, whom the Father will send in my name, will teach you all things and will remind you of everything I have said to you" (John 14:26).

Emotions play a key role in this process because they often are an important indication that some part of our life needs to change. That is why the last chapter described emotions as a window into the soul. This is also why Paul says, "Examine yourselves to see whether you are in the faith; test yourselves" (2 Corinthians 13:5) and "Each one should test his own actions" (Galatians 6:4). When we do this with a genuinely seeking heart, God reveals to us what we need to know and points us in the direction that He wants us to go.

This process of being made holy by the power and will of God is called sanctification. I can give no scientific explanation for it since it is by definition a spiritual process. In some mysterious way, when your spirit is joined to God's Spirit through Christ, a process begins that involves the interaction of your physical body, mind, and spirit with God's Holy Spirit that begins an inner transformation that Christians have testified about for two thousand years.

As you yield to the process of sanctification, your body, mind, and spirit progressively come under the influence of the Holy Spirit, giving you an ever deeper understanding of both yourself and God. As you let God heal past hurts and change your thinking, your emotions begin to work in closer conjunction with your intellect to help you know when you are in God's will. You also begin to see how your emotions reveal those aspects of yourself that still need to be surrendered to God's healing touch. This healing not only includes how you think, but can even change deep-seated automatic emotional responses that have caused problems in the past.

▶RECOMMENDED ACTIVITIES

CHECK YOUR MORAL COMPASS

This chapter discussed how God is very clear about His will. The clearest statement of it is the Ten Commandments in Exodus 20:1–17. Over the next ten days, take one commandment each day and think about what it means and how well you conform to it. Take at least fifteen minutes each day to do the following.

- Start with prayer and ask God to open your heart and mind to the truths about both the commandment and yourself that He wants to reveal to you.
- If you have any study materials that deal with the commandment, take a few minutes to read them. If you have Internet access, you might find it useful to look up two or three sermons on the commandment you are meditating on that day.[1]
- Ask yourself the following:
  - In my own words, what is this commandment saying?
  - How does this apply to life in today's world?
  - How does this apply to me?
  - In what ways do I conform to this commandment?
  - In what ways am I not conforming to it?
  - What changes do I need to make to more fully conform to it?
- Thank God for insights He gives you and ask for His help in carrying out any actions He wants you to take.

---

1 The easiest way to locate sermons on a specific commandment is to go to a search engine such as Google and enter the verse or verses that state the commandment enclosed in quotation marks. Then place the word "sermon" outside the quotation marks. Here is an example of what you would type if you were looking for sermons on the first commandment:

"Exodus 20:3" sermon

Get "Plugged in" to Christ's Body

The Recommended Activities of chapter 2 discussed the importance of being an active member of a Spirit-filled church. If you are not attending a church regularly, make the commitment this week to begin regular attendance at a Bible centered church. If you are already attending a church regularly but are not participating in any kind of small group, identify one that appeals to you and begin attending it regularly.

Get Wisdom

This chapter discusses how God has already made His will known through the Bible. It also discusses how solutions for most of the problems you face in life have already been addressed there. If you are not reading the Bible regularly, begin doing so now. If you are not sure how to begin, ask your pastor or a Christian friend to help you. You may find it useful to use one of the many Bible reading guides or daily devotionals that are available.

Continue to Reflect on What Your Emotions Reveal about Your Spiritual Character

The Recommended Activities for chapter 7 outlined a way to look at events and see how they reveal your true spiritual character. When you experience upsets, continue to take some time to use the process outlined in chapter 7 to uncover what they say about your spiritual character.

CHAPTER 9

HOW GOD SPEAKS TO YOU

"Hear, O LORD, and answer me, for I am poor and needy" (Psalm 86:1). So begins a plea whose words would sound familiar to countless people throughout history. Praise be to God that as Christians, we have the promise that we can go to God when we face difficult decisions, and He will guide us: "If any of you lacks wisdom, he should ask God, who gives generously to all without finding fault, and it will be given to him" (James 1:5). Why is it, then, that so often we hear fellow believers say, "I wish God would just tell me what to do!"? The answer: They don't know how to listen.

This chapter looks at the different ways God speaks to you, methods to increase your ability to hear Him, and the role emotions play in both blocking your ability to hear God as well as helping you know when He is talking to you.

FIVE THINGS THAT PREVENT YOU FROM HEARING GOD

God is always willing to make His will known to you. However, there are several things that can keep you from hearing His voice. Let's look at five of the most common ones.

Unrenounced Sin

When conscious and unrenounced sin is in your life, God's Spirit will not point forward but will continue to point back to the festering sin until you repent and move in a new direction that matches God's moral will. The principle is simple: un-renounced sin separates you from God. This is stated in several different ways in the Bible. Isaiah 59:2 states: "Your iniquities have separated you from your God; your sins have hidden his face from you, so that he will not hear." Psalm 66:18 says, "If I had cherished sin in my heart, the LORD would not have listened." Sinful behavior is clearly described in the Bible. The best-known list of behaviors that are approved of and forbidden by God is the Ten Commandments.

Jesus deepened our understanding of sin by describing how the source of all sin is a person's heart: "From within, out of men's hearts, come evil thoughts, sexual immorality, theft, murder, adultery, greed, malice, deceit, lewdness, envy, slander, arrogance and folly" (Mark 7:21–22). Each of these types of sin is usually accompanied by negative emotions such as anger, resentment, lust, envy, anxiety, or fear. Whenever you experience one of these emotions, it is time to identify what is generating it. Would God approve of the thoughts and desires generating the emotion? Or rather, do you already know they are contrary to what God wants? If so, ask for forgiveness and help in changing your heart and mind so you can see the situation as God sees it.

As you acknowledge sin, repent, and approach God with a clean conscience and pure heart, you begin to see and hear God clearly (Matthew 5:8).

Unforgiveness

Unforgiveness comes in many forms, such as bitterness, hatred, malice, holding grudges, and resentment. With each of these, the underlying emotion is anger and a desire to see the person who wronged you punished in some way. To make matters worse, because our human nature and the wisdom of the world tell us that we should get even when we are wronged, we often feel justified in feeling this way. However, this is not the way of God.

Jesus offered himself up as a sacrifice so that we can live in grace. God expects us to offer that same grace to others. That is why the "root of bitterness" (Hebrews 12:15, NASB, KJV), springing from an unforgiving heart blocks the fruit of the Holy Spirit and stunts your spiritual growth. Scripture is very clear on this point:

> If you forgive men when they sin against you, your heavenly Father will also forgive you. But if you do not forgive men their sins, your Father will not forgive your sins. (Matthew 6:14–15)

> When you stand praying, if you hold anything against anyone, forgive him, so that your Father in heaven may forgive you your sins. (Mark 11:25)

> Be kind and compassionate to one another, forgiving each other, just as in Christ God forgave you. (Ephesians 4:32)

When you have been given clear instruction, you need to be willing to do what God wants even when it doesn't seem to make sense and goes against everything you are feeling inside.

If you have been holding onto bitter feelings towards someone, you may find that releasing your resentment and forgiving this person is the key to developing the spiritual relationship with God that you are seeking. It will also open the door to the peace and joy you were meant to have.

For deep seated resentments, especially those dealing with childhood wounds, this often takes time. You may even need to talk to your pastor or a Christian counselor if you are finding it difficult to release a resentment that has been part of your life for many years. However, the renewed spirit, peace, joy, and dynamic relationship with God that you gain are well worth it.

Wrong Priorities

Jesus said: "No one can serve two masters. Either he will hate the one and love the other, or he will be devoted to the one and despise the other. You cannot serve both God and Money" (Matthew 6:24). John described the folly of putting other things before God this way:

> Do not love the world or anything in the world. If anyone loves the world, the love of the Father is not in him. For everything in the world—the cravings of sinful man, the lust of his eyes and the boasting of what he has and does—comes not from the Father but from the world. The world and its desires pass away, but the man who does the will of God lives forever. (1 John 2:15–17)

The Greek phrase translated as the "cravings of sinful man" is literally, "the desires or longings of the flesh" and refers to sexual desires and sensuality—the things that satisfy the flesh. We live in a society where the satisfying of sexual desires and sensual pleasures such as food, drink, and entertainment are often presented as the ultimate goal in life. The "lust [or longings] of the eyes" refers to those things that you see and want. Again, advertising presents an endless parade of things that it claims will make us happy. The "pride of life" refers to a pride or arrogance based on your possessions or accomplishments. This pride reflects a refusal to acknowledge that all of your abilities and possessions are a gift from God.

Jesus stated it clearly:

> Anyone who loves his father or mother more than me is not worthy of me; anyone who loves his son or daughter more than me is not worthy of me; and anyone who does not take his cross and follow me is not worthy of me. Whoever finds his life will lose it, and whoever loses his life for my sake will find it. (Matthew 10:37–39)

It is only when you make God your first priority and are willing to act on what He is telling you that you are able to understand clearly what He is saying to you. When God is second, third, or fourth on your list of priorities, His voice is lost in the clamor of worldly things demanding your ear.

Separation from Christ's Body

Fellowshipping and developing deep relationships with other believers are two of the most powerful ways to increase your faith and learn about yourself and God. That is why Hebrews instructs us to "consider how we may spur one another on toward love and good deeds. Let us not give up meeting together, as some are in the habit of doing, but let us encourage one another—and all the more as you see the Day approaching" (Hebrews 10:24–25).

Because the church is Christ's body, it has been given prophets, evangelists, pastors, and teachers (Ephesians 4:11). Paul says that all these have been given for a purpose:

Then we will no longer be infants, tossed back and forth by the waves, and blown here and there by every wind of teaching and by the cunning and craftiness of men in their deceitful scheming. Instead, speaking the truth in love, we will in all things grow up into him who is the Head, that is, Christ. From him the whole body, joined and held together by every supporting ligament, grows and builds itself up in love, as each part does its work. (Ephesians 4:14–16)

If you are having difficulty hearing what God is telling you, it may simply be that you are not in the place where He often speaks most clearly. Being connected to the church means you are connected to Christ's body. This is a resource God provides to help you become spiritually mature so that you might bear much fruit for God's kingdom.

Neglect of the Spiritual Disciplines

Many Christians see spiritual disciplines as a relic from the past that simply do not fit into the modern lifestyle. At the same time, they also usually find that little growth has taken place in their lives after years of claiming to follow Christ. Worse yet, they are not experiencing the close personal relationship with God that we were meant to have. The answer to this dilemma is to take a fresh look at what is meant by spiritual disciplines.

While there is no agreed-upon list of spiritual disciplines, many things are frequently mentioned. More important, it is generally agreed that the purpose of a spiritual discipline is to turn your heart and mind away from worldly things and towards God. Because of this, it is essential that anything you choose to do should be done out of a heart-felt desire to know God better and draw closer to Him rather than out of a sense of obligation or for some special reward. Spiritual disciplines done out of obligation or to obtain a specific blessing, usually become an empty practice and may even lead to resentment toward God.

Spiritual disciplines can include many different types of practices. Here are several that are most frequently mentioned.

Prayer

Of all the disciplines, prayer is the most foundational. Taking time for daily personal prayer opens up your spiritual channels and helps center your mind on God in a way that nothing else can do. If you've never practiced taking time daily to talk to God, useful suggestions can be found in Appendix 2: Suggestions on Prayer.

Bible Study

The previous chapter discussed how God has already spoken many things to us through His Word, the Bible. Do not expect Him to tell you more if you have not bothered to listen to what He has already told you.

Meditation/Quiet Time

Although there are many different formal types of Christian meditation, the simplest form is to take regular time to reflect on spiritual matters. During this time you can think about a passage of scripture you have read or studied, Sunday's sermon, or how God views a life issue you are facing.

Fasting

Possibly nothing runs so counter to our modern culture's desire for immediate need gratification as self-denial. However, the purpose of fasting is to help us turn our minds and hearts towards God by giving up something of the world for a period of time. Fasting does not need to be limited to not eating or drinking. It also includes giving up some activity you value, such as watching television or a particular food that you like, such as chocolate. Many good books and Internet sites offer suggestions on how to use fasting to draw closer to God.

Other Disciplines

Many other activities both private and corporate are described by various people as spiritual disciplines. Some of the most frequently mentioned ones are stewardship, service, worship, journaling, retreats, and pilgrimages. In addition, many of the spiritual disciplines can be combined such as prayer and fasting.

If you feel that your spiritual life is flat and joyless, selecting one or two of the spiritual disciplines to practice may be the key to experiencing a deeper relationship with God and an increased ability to hear what He is saying to you.

WAYS IN WHICH GOD SPEAKS TO YOU

God speaks to us in a variety of ways. Trying to put them into neat categories is difficult, since several of the categories often overlap. Keeping this in mind, here are the five most common ways in which God speaks to you.

The Bible

In the Bible, God has said a great deal through many different authors over the course of thousands of years. He expects you to learn and listen to what He has already said. Indeed, most of the answers you are seeking are already there. Often, simply knowing and applying the basic teachings and examples in the Bible provide all the guidance you need in a given situation.

As you read and study the Bible, God uses what you've learned to communicate to you through your thoughts, your emotions, and other people.

Thoughts

God will often put thoughts in our minds. This is especially true for those who read the Bible regularly. He does this in three ways:

During times of trouble or temptation, God will often bring to mind Bible verses or stories that comfort and strengthen you and point you in the direction He wants you to go.

When you are seeking guidance in prayer, God will often bring to mind scriptures that are the key to answering your question. If you are a new Christian (or have not done much Bible study) and are not sure where in the Bible to look for answers, ask a pastor or fellow believer who lives a godly life and knows the Bible to help you find Bible passages that address your issue.

When you read Scripture with a seeking heart, God opens up its meaning to you in new and personal ways. It is a common testimony that during times of uncertainty, a particular verse that holds the answer seems to jump off the page as one reads.

An Emotional Response to a Song or Teaching

God often speaks to us through our emotions. While you are listening to a sermon, worshiping God in song, or participating in a Bible study, something that is said strikes you in a powerful way and gives you a message that you need to hear whether it is a word of comfort, direction, warning, rebuke, or encouragement.

Other People

God often speaks through His body, the church. By the church I do not mean a particular denomination, but rather, those fellow Christians who make up the community where you worship. The

Holy Spirit has endowed your fellow believers with a wide variety of gifts. Among these gifts, "To one there is given through the Spirit the message of wisdom, to another the message of knowledge by means of the same Spirit" (1 Corinthians 12:8).[2] The Bible also frequently repeats the advice: "Plans fail for lack of counsel, but with many advisers they succeed" (Proverbs 15:22).

When you are dealing with a difficult situation or need to make an important decision, it is easy to be blinded by personal desires or strong emotions. Godly men and women who are not involved, gifted, and mature in faith can view your situation more objectively and apply the principles of Scripture with a clearer eye.

Supernatural Ways

God can and does speak directly to people in supernatural ways. However, this is the *least common* way in which God speaks to believers since He has so many other ways to communicate with us. Unfortunately, many Christians become overly enamored with testimonies of this type of communication. While seeking supernatural communication, they often ignore God's more usual ways of communicating.

Supernatural communication from God generally takes one of three forms. The first is when a person, by means of the Holy Spirit, speaks a word into your life as a result of the gift of prophecy. When this happens, be willing to hear what God is saying. Paul warns, "Do not put out the Spirit's fire; do not treat prophecies with contempt" (1 Thessalonians 5:19-20). At the same time, in the next verse, he adds, "Test everything." Weigh what you are told against Scripture. Just because someone says, "God told me to tell you . . . " it doesn't automatically mean that it is God talking.

---

2 Additional gifts are listed in 1 Corinthians 12:1–11; Romans 12:6–8; and 1 Peter 4:10–11.

A second form of supernatural communication comes in the form of a strong impression to do something. Cricket, a friend of mine offers a good example of this. She loves the Lord dearly and has a very rich prayer life. Sometimes, she tells me about something that she strongly felt that she had to do. It seemed illogical at the time but was clearly an impression by the Holy Spirit. Sometimes it is as simple as the thought that she needs to pray for or call someone she may not even know very well. It usually turns out later that this person was facing a difficult situation at that moment or needed encouragement.

One of the more dramatic instances involved her son, who is profoundly disabled. One evening she felt the Lord telling her very strongly to get her son to the hospital immediately. He did not have a fever and showed no signs of any problems. Because she knew that her son's special needs required a pediatrician, she went to the emergency room and demanded that one see him immediately. After the doctor examined the boy, he asked her why she had brought him to the hospital. She simply said, "God told me to." He then told her that her son did need immediate attention. In fact, he said that if she had arrived fifteen minutes later her son would have probably died.

On rare occasions, God will speak to a person with an audible voice, through visions and dreams, or through the visitation of an angel. Lana, another friend and sincere Christian lady, recently told our small group about an incident when her younger daughter was a toddler. Lana was combing her hair as her husband, Chris, was in the car getting ready to leave. Suddenly, she had a vision of Chris backing over the child. She rushed out of the house and saw the child getting ready to walk behind the vehicle in a blind spot where Chris would not have seen her. Lana rescued her daughter and no harm was done. This daughter is now a wonderful young Christian lady who is touching many lives.

While the experiences of Cricket and Lana are powerful demonstrations of God's supernatural communication, they are unusual experiences. People who have experiences like these may have only one during their whole life. Others might have several. People I know who have had such experiences share one thing in common: they have spent much time with the Lord. Jesus said, "I am the good shepherd; I know my sheep and my sheep know me" (John 10:14). A little later He said, "My sheep listen to my voice; I know them, and they follow me" (verse 27). Don't expect to be able to hear God's voice if you don't spend time with Him.

A Word of Warning

Because it is so easy for us to deceive ourselves, an important word of warning applies to each of these methods that God uses to talk to us. True godly counsel always lines up with what has already been spoken, the Bible. If you feel that God is telling you to do something, be careful and test your spiritual leadings against the Word of God. If you are not sure, talk with people who have a close relationship with God and know the Bible well. As you draw closer to God and understand His Word more deeply, you know more clearly whether a thought or impression is simply a personal desire or truly His leading.

▶Recommended Activities

Identify Things that Are Preventing You from Hearing God

Read through the section titled, "Five Things that Prevent You from Hearing God." Put a check mark by any that you feel applies to you. In addition, consider the past few weeks and answer the following questions:

- Is there sin in my life that I am aware of but refuse to renounce because I enjoy it too much or am addicted to it?
- Have I experienced negative emotions such as anger, resentment, lust, envy, anxiety, or fear? If so, what provoked these feelings?
- Is there someone I have not forgiven or need to ask for forgiveness?
- Have I felt anger towards someone for some wrong I believe he or she did?
- When I look at how I spend my time and money, what is most important to me?
- Are there things in the world that I love more than God?
- Is there some "right" that I think I have that keeps me from submitting to God?
- Do I practice any of the spiritual disciplines described in this chapter? If so, is my practice consistent or hit-and-miss?

After answering these questions, decide what action you might need to take. Share your plan with a fellow believer you trust who is mature in Christ.

CHECK YOUR "SPIRITUAL EARS"

After you have spent a few days with the previous exercise take a few days to assess whether or not you are listening to God. One of the best ways to assess your "spiritual ears" is to look at how you make decisions. Begin by reading the section titled, "Ways in which God Speaks to You" at least twice. Then make a list of the various types of decisions you have had to make during the past few months. After you've composed the list, ask yourself the following questions:

- Did I take time to identify what the Bible has to say about any of these situations? If I don't know the Bible well, did I ask for help from someone I trust?
- Did I pray about it? By this I mean, not a simple one- or two-sentence prayer, but prayer where you:
  - Examine the situation from several different perspectives,
  - Ponder how to apply Scripture to this situation,
  - Consider counsel you have received, and
  - Ask God not only to give you wisdom, but to reveal things about either yourself or the situation that you need to know or change.
- Did I seek counsel from a godly person?
- Were there open doors (opportunities) that I ignored?
- What role did my emotions play in making either a poor or a wise decision?
- Did the actions that I decided on bring a sense of peace in my heart and mind?

Be sure to record your observations and any insights in your journal.

CHAPTER 10

EMOTIONS THAT COME OUT OF THE BLUE

The circumstances that trigger most of our emotions are easy to identify. You win a prize. A car cuts you off in traffic, nearly causing an accident. You see an old friend. Someone you love ignores you. You successfully complete a difficult project. A friend makes fun of you in a hurtful way. However, we sometimes experience emotions that seem mysterious and cause us to wonder, "Where did that come from?"

For example, Kim receives an e-mail from her supervisor saying he wants to talk with her. While it would be understandable to be a little nervous, Kim experiences overwhelming fear as she thinks about the upcoming meeting. She doesn't understand why she is reacting this way, since she is good at what she does and knows that he probably just wants to talk about a routine issue.

Raymond is engaged to a young lady he has been seeing for some time. Then, when they are alone and feeling close, she casually mentions that she wonders how he would look with his hair a little different. Raymond finds himself becoming angry and complaining about how she is never satisfied with things as they are. Afterwards, he wonders why he was so angry about something so insignificant.

In this chapter we'll take a look at something called conditioned emotional responses which often seem to appear "out of the blue." We'll also look at how the subjective, physical, mental, and spiritual aspects of emotions are intertwined.

Conditioned Emotional Responses

At the beginning of the twentieth century, I. P. Pavlov conducted what is now a classic experiment. He would let a dog hear a bell ring then immediately place meat powder on the dog's tongue, causing it to salivate. After he had repeated this many times, the sound of the bell alone would cause the dog to salivate. Pavlov called the salivation of the dog in response to the bell a *conditioned response*. This process of associating a reflex response (salivation) with a stimulus that is normally unrelated to it (the sound of the bell) is now known as *classical* or *Pavlovian conditioning*.

Conditioned emotional responses are similar to classical conditioning. The difference is that instead of triggering a simple reflex response like salivation, the stimulus now becomes the trigger for an emotional response. Kim provides a good example of this. She was a child with a gentle and compliant spirit who was raised in a home with strict parents who became very angry when they disciplined her. When this happened, Kim would become frightened and immediately comply with whatever her parents wanted. Over time, Kim's amygdalae (as discussed in detail in chapter 3) stamped the repeated experiences of disapproving looks and voices of her parents as dangerous. In response, she learned to calm the intense anxiety triggered by her parents' disapproval by becoming submissive and doing whatever she felt was needed to regain their approval.

This response carried over into Kim's adult life. Whenever she experienced disapproval from others, she reacted with intense anxiety. This emotional response then triggered the protective behaviors she had learned in childhood: suppressing her emotions and being compliant. Even the thought of receiving disapproval would trigger this response. This is what happened when she received the email from her supervisor. Her first thought was, "Did I do something wrong?" Emotionally, the thought of her supervisor correcting a possible mistake felt like she was going to be admonished by her parents.

Raymond provides an example of how a child with parents who were overly harsh like Kim's can develop quite a different response. Raymond was raised in a home with a very critical mother and a father who was quick to become angry. His parents often had loud arguments. However, unlike Kim, Raymond was an assertive and strong-willed child. Instead of becoming quiet and compliant when his mother made critical remarks about him, Raymond would respond with anger that mirrored his father's behavior. When Raymond's fiancée made the remark about his hair, it felt, on an unconscious emotional level, the same as when his mother criticized him. This triggered the anger that was associated with criticism and the automatic lashing out that he had learned from his father.

Conditioned emotional responses explain many of the intense emotional reactions people experience that seem to appear unexpectedly or out of proportion to what would normally be expected in a given situation. The mysterious quality they have is due to the brain's amazing ability to track and interpret, at an unconscious level that you are never aware of, the many complex events taking place around you (as discussed in chapter 3). This ability is what makes conditioned responses seem to just "come out of the blue." In the same way, the behaviors that these emotions trigger are automatic responses that developed after years of practice during childhood.

Up to now, I have focused on negative conditioned responses. However, there is also a positive side to them. Conditioned emotional responses explain many of the positive emotional reactions we have as well as some of the behaviors we use to comfort ourselves. For example, Kim's mother would often reward her with Chinese almond cookies. For a gentle spirit like Kim, her mother's approval was especially important. Receiving a cookie from her mother became an important sign that she was loved. As an adult, when Kim went into a market that specialized in Asian foods, she would find herself drawn to the almond cookies. Purchasing and eating one gave her a feeling of comfort. Sometimes, when she was feeling bad, she would buy some to cheer herself up.

It turns out that the combination of classical conditioning and conditioned emotional responses plays a major, though usually unrecognized, role in your daily life. Many of your preferences and dislikes are the result of the conditioning you experienced when you were young. A good example is the food you like to eat. That is why you enjoy food you are familiar with and often do not like food that is different from what you know. The sights, odors, and tastes of food you are familiar with trigger a positive response when you are hungry, but the sights, odors, and tastes of unfamiliar foods or spices may produce the opposite reaction. Just the sight of people eating some foods, such as snakes, grubs, or insects, may even sicken you while others might find their mouths watering at the sight of such delicacies. The same can be said of the music you enjoy as well as many aspects of how you approach work and what you find entertaining.

IDENTIFYING CONDITIONED EMOTIONAL RESPONSES

Because conditioned emotional responses connected to danger are important for our survival, they can be especially strong. This explains why people who have grown up in harsh circumstances often have strong conditioned emotional responses connected to those things that were painful or dangerous when they were young. With both Kim and Raymond, the conditioned emotional responses we looked at involved disapproval from their parents. However, many other types of conditioned emotional responses can develop.

A person who experienced repeated sexual abuse can develop conditioned emotional responses that interfere with intimacy later in life. A person who grew up with physical abuse or in a society devastated by war can develop a wide range of conditioned emotional responses associated with physical safety, food, or shelter.

Take a moment to reflect on how you react to the following:

- People in authority
- People who are loud and boisterous
- People who are timid and shy
- People of the same sex who are attractive
- People of the same sex who are not attractive
- People of the opposite sex who are attractive
- People of the opposite sex who are not attractive
- People who are in physical or emotional pain
- Situations involving success, failure, or death

- Situations where events are occurring that are out of your control
- Situations where there is a threat
- Situations where events are not predictable
- Situations involving intimacy
- Situations where tenderness or love is being expressed
- Situations where you are being teased or criticized

If any of these tend to trigger emotions that seem illogical or out of proportion to circumstances, it is possible that a conditioned emotional response is present. For many, the easiest way to identify the source of the conditioned emotional response is to ask oneself: "What situation or circumstances from my past triggered the same emotional response that I experienced in this situation?" In Kim's case, she immediately saw that the fear she felt when her parents criticized or scolded her was the same as her reaction to her supervisor. In Raymond's case, the connection did not come as easily.

Raymond had two negative core beliefs that interfered with his ability to see himself clearly: "I need to always be strong" and "I don't make mistakes." Because of this, he initially would justify his response by saying it was due to his fiancée's insensitivity. Yet, he knew deep inside that this wasn't true. As I asked him to think about his childhood and identify times when he had reacted in a similar manner, he soon realized that this was the same reaction he had towards his mother whenever she criticized him. With more reflection he realized that he had modeled this behavior on that of his father.

LOOKING AT THE WHOLE ELEPHANT

So far, we have looked at the four different aspects of emotions —subjective, physical, mental, and spiritual—separately. Conditioned emotional responses provide us with the opportunity to look at how these four different aspects interact. Borrowing from the parable of the blind men and the elephant introduced in the first chapter, it is time to step back and look at the whole elephant. At first glance, it might seem that conditioned emotional responses only involve the subjective and physical aspects of emotions. However, even simple responses like the two described at the beginning of this chapter develop in the context of emerging core beliefs and a spiritual atmosphere that affect how the response develops and which are in turn themselves affected by the development of the response.

Kim's gentle personality and childhood experiences with overly harsh parents produced core beliefs about being inferior and unable to do anything right. Her fearful conditioned response to authority figures and the behaviors associated with it were shaped by these beliefs and reinforced them. All this further became intertwined with two spiritual issues that limited her ability to have a rich and dynamic relationship with God.

While working with this seemingly simple conditioned emotional response, Kim realized that fear of her parents had distorted her image of God. She often envisioned God as an angry parent just waiting for her to make a mistake so He could punish her. This image often caused unnecessary guilt and shame and kept her from experiencing the joy that the Christian life is meant to bring. This distorted image also made it difficult for Kim to trust God and believe that He really cared for her.

This part of her spiritual life took a long time to heal. The first step was the simple realization that her experiences with her earthly parents had colored her relationship with her heavenly Father. However, as we have discussed previously, there is a big difference between knowing something and having an experiential understanding of it.

In a book like this, it's impossible to list all the things that helped Kim see herself through God's eyes. Over several months, Kim prayed regularly for God to help her separate Him from her parents and feel safe with Him. As she struggled with this issue, the Holy Spirit opened up several passages of Scripture that had never really had much meaning for her. One verse that spoke to her in a personal way was John 3:1: "How great is the love the Father has lavished on us, that we should be called children of God! And that is what we are!" She memorized the verse and found that it encouraged and comforted her when she was feeling weak and insignificant.

Equally important was the development of close relationships with fellow believers in her church who had loving hearts and a strong and positive relationship with God. Through them she experienced what unconditional love felt like. Over time she saw that her gentle nature was not a curse but a gift that God wanted her to share with others. Experiences with fellow believers who were hurting showed her that her tender and loving nature allowed her to minister in ways that others couldn't. At the same time, she found that, with God's help, she could indeed be bold when she needed to. Over time, all these experiences combined to change her image of God and enabled her to feel at a subjective level the love that God has for her.

Whenever you ask God to help you with a personal issue and pray about it regularly, you find that God presents an array of opportunities for you to stretch and grow. He also provides the resources you need to make the most of each opportunity if you are willing to step out in faith. One example from Kim's journey occurred when she was asked to help at the information table at her church on Sundays. This was a big step for her; she did not like dealing with strangers because she might do something stupid or they might look down on her. However, she believed that God was leading her to do this so she asked God to give her courage and wisdom. As she saw how God gave her words to say and touch people in a positive way, she gained confidence in the fact that God had created her to be a treasured part of the body of Christ.

Like Kim, Raymond found that the simple conditioned emotional response he was dealing with was associated with negative core beliefs about what it meant to be a man. In addition, he identified spiritual issues concerning his self-sufficiency and the pride he took in his intellect and talents. These attitudes and beliefs made it difficult for Raymond to acknowledge his shortcomings. However, as he began to work with his angry conditioned response to criticism, the Holy Spirit used it to humble him and show him how much he needed God. While wrestling with this issue, he also learned how important it is to see gifts and talents that we've been given not as something we developed on our own, but as something God has blessed us with and helped us develop so we can bless others.

One of the most important experiences that helped Raymond was to see how powerful prayer was. On days when Raymond skipped his morning devotional, he began to see how easily he slipped back into old patterns. On days when he spent time praying and asking God to help him respond in a way that was pleasing to God, Raymond found that his behavior changed. While he had belonged to a church for many years, this experience was the key to moving him from a lackluster faith to a new and dynamic relationship with God.

What's Happening, What's Real

A simple yet powerful way to diminish conditioned emotional responses is to use a two-step approach that I developed early in my practice while working with people who had been traumatized.

Step 1: Identify Situations that Trigger the Conditioned Emotional Response

The more clearly you identify both your reaction and the situations that trigger it, the more successful you will be. With Kim it was clear that her reaction to her supervisor was a conditioned emotional response that had developed as a result of the fear she experienced whenever her parents were angry. However, as she thought about it, she recalled many incidents where teachers and people who she considered to be strong or authoritative would trigger the same response.

Step 2: Tell Yourself What's Happening and What's Real

Kim developed the following statement that she could read whenever the thoughts about meeting with her supervisor made her anxious:

> "*What's happening* is that I am experiencing a conditioned emotional response that was due to my being frightened of my parent's anger.
>
> *What's real* is that I am going to see my supervisor. He is not my parent. He is just my supervisor. I am safe. We are going to discuss routine office business. He is not going to yell at me or hit me. He is always very professional and likes my work. These feelings are just leftovers from the past. They will diminish over time. God, help me know in my inner being that "I can do everything through him who gives me strength" (Philippians 4:13) and that "the Lord is with me; I will not be afraid. What can man do to me?" (Psalm 118:6).

As Kim practiced talking to herself in this manner, she found that after several months her supervisor no longer triggered the exaggerated fear that she used to experience. She also began to feel the power and presence of the Holy Spirit in her life in a new and wonderful way.

Conditioned emotional responses are usually connected to beliefs and spiritual issues that need to be healed. Whenever you identify a conditioned emotional response that interferes with your life, take time to identify unbiblical beliefs you hold as well as what this response says about your relationship to God. While the "what's happening, what's real" technique can help diminish the strength of the response, complete healing often only comes when the core beliefs and spiritual issues associated with it are addressed.

While it is possible to reach a point where old responses become dormant, the "wiring" that triggers them is still present. Occasionally, people find that they do recur. Usually, this is when a person is sick, stressed, or facing a major life challenge. At these times you may have to go through the same steps you took when you first were working with the response. The good news is that relearning is always easier than the original learning. These times when you dip into old patterns are also opportunities that God uses to move you to a new spiritual level, if you allow Him to guide you.

In Kim's case, she found that even though her reaction to her supervisor quieted, there were still occasional times when her response would be activated by a strong personality or a situation where there was uncertainty. At times like these she found that rephrasing her "what's happening, what's real" statement in a spiritual manner greatly increased its effectiveness. Here is an example of the type of self-talk she would use:

> *Dear God, I know that what I'm experiencing now is the result of having earthly parents who did not know You and who were very broken and frightening to me as a child. Heal*

*this area of my mind and spirit, and help me know that You
love me and are guiding me in this situation. I affirm with
Paul, 'I can do everything through him who gives me strength'
(Philippians 4:13).*

When Raymond realized that he was responding to his fiancé as
if she were his mother, he began to do two things. First, he reminded
himself regularly that he needed to be quiet when he became angry
and take time to cool down. At first, he even found that he needed to
excuse himself so he would not repeat his old behavior. As he calmed
down he would use the "what's happening, what's real" approach.
Here is an example of the type of self-talk he used:

*While growing up, I learned from my dad that you shoot first
and ask questions later. As a teen, I copied my dad's behavior
and would become angry and say mean things to Mom when
she criticized me. My fiancé is not my mother. She loves me
very much and was not acting like my mother. It only felt like
it because I'm so sensitive to being criticized by a woman.
What she said was simply her way of trying to help me. It was
not meant as a criticism.*

As Raymond worked with this response, he found, like Kim,
that it pointed to a spiritual need. First, he realized that he still
had a lot of resentment towards both his parents and needed to
forgive them for the mistakes they had made. He also realized that
he could be both angry like his father and critical like his mother.
By discussing this with a Christian counselor, he came to see his
parents as having been damaged by their own childhoods.

Eventually, Raymond's resentment changed to sadness over the
brokenness of the world that was reflected in them and the many
lost blessings that could have been. In addition to counseling,

Raymond found that prayer and being involved in a small-group Bible study were essential for his healing. He found it helpful to discuss his struggles with others who had similar backgrounds. Like Kim, he also found that adding the spiritual dimension to the "what's happening, what's real" approach made it much more powerful. He would say things such as this:

> *"The old pattern of becoming angry has just been triggered. God, I know that You are more powerful than this pattern. Thank You for helping me break this pattern and for healing the brokenness of my parents that was passed to me. Help me now see my fiancée with Your eyes and respond with love. Cleanse me of the anger that Satan has used to keep me in bondage in the past."*

IF IT'S NOT BROKEN, IT DOESN'T NEED FIXING

After reading the initial draft of this chapter, a friend of mine commented that he was having a difficult time identifying the types of negative conditioned emotional responses described in the chapter. This person came from a very loving Christian home and has known Christ all his life. His wife comes from a similar background. Though they have faced difficulties, they have not experienced the types of trauma that several of the examples describe.

If this is true for you, you probably do not have any major negative conditioned emotional responses. However, you can still probably identify areas of your life where conditioned emotional responses are triggered. Many of these will be positive, such as a warm sense of peace when you see your church or a happy expectation when you are about to engage in a treasured family tradition. Some will involve an appropriate response to things that are destructive, such as anger when someone is hurting another person or sadness when a person is engaging in self-destructive behavior. This is the way conditioned emotional responses were intended to work.

If you don't identify negative conditioned emotional responses, it may simply mean that this is not a problem for you. However, you can still look around and see lots of examples of how they interfere with the lives of people you know. Knowing this can help you be more compassionate when you see them reacting in what appears to be an irrational manner.

As in previous chapters, the examples in this and the next chapter involve people who come from difficult backgrounds. They provide clear examples of conditioned emotional responses that are causing problems. While everyone has conditioned emotional responses of one type or another, many do not have the intense negative ones that cause problems.

▶Recommended Activities

Ask God to Help You See any Conditioned Emotional Responses that You Need to Address

Because we are masters at self-deception, it is often difficult to see just where growth is needed. If you are not aware of any conditioned emotional responses that you need to address, ask God to reveal to you any that you need to be aware of. Don't just do this once, but continue for a week before moving on. If you become aware of a problem conditioned emotional response, use the ideas in this chapter to address the response along with the beliefs and spiritual issues associated with it.

Be sure to review the lists of worldly beliefs in chapter 5 and negative core beliefs in chapter 6. If your behavior corresponds to one or more of these beliefs, you need to address it.

If you have already identified a conditioned emotional response that is causing problems, be sure to ask for God's help in applying the ideas in this chapter.

Look at the Roots of Your Emotional Responses

While your genetic wiring plays a role in the way you currently manage your emotions, the habits you developed while growing up are equally important. For most people, this is a mixed bag of both positive and negative experiences. The result is that they manage some emotions well and manage others poorly. In this exercise, it is equally important to identify strengths as well as weaknesses.

Identify responses that were modeled after the people who raised you.
- How did the people who raised me manage anger, fear, disappointment, sadness, and hurt?
- How did they express joy, excitement, hope, tenderness, and love?
- What do I do that is similar to what they did?

Identify how the way you managed emotions when you were young benefited you.
- How did your place in the family (status, birth order, role, etc.) shape the way you managed your emotions?
- How did the way you managed your emotions either protect you or provide you with attention?

Identify conditioned emotional responses.

- Have there been any times in the past few weeks when you've responded to a situation with inappropriate emotions?
- If so, what actions did you take? Were you able to act in an appropriate manner in spite of them or not?
- Would any of these occurrences be considered a conditioned emotional response?

Identify associated beliefs and spiritual issues.

- What worldly beliefs are connected to this response? (Review the lists in chapters 5 and 6.)
- Is there a spiritual issue that this response is pointing to? If so, what?

DEVELOP A "WHAT'S HAPPENING, WHAT'S REAL" STATEMENT

Write a simple "what's happening, what's real" statement for any conditioned emotional response you identify. Follow the pattern described in this chapter. After you have written your statement, take time to pray about this response and the circumstances that generated it. Ask God to reveal to you any areas of your spiritual life that are damaged as a result of the circumstances that created this conditioned emotional response.

Several questions you can answer to help in this process are listed below. When answering them, do not give the "correct" answer, the one you think you should give; instead, describe the beliefs about God that are reflected in your behavior and the emotional reactions. As discussed in Chapter 7, these are the true window into your soul.

- Is God Safe?
- Is God really a loving God?
- Does God actually care about me?
- Can I trust God?
- Does God have my best interests at heart?
- Do I keep control over my life, or do I submit to God's control?
- Do I rely on my own strength or on God when I'm facing challenges?

Keep in mind that a spiritual wound might linger for several weeks or months, sometimes years, before you feel it has been healed. How quickly it takes depends on how willing you are to look at the issue, how completely you submit yourself and your need to God, and how committed you are to discovering and following what the Bible has to say about this issue. If you are struggling with deep-seated issues that are seriously interfering with your life, you may need help from a pastor or counselor. Keep in mind that they are often instruments that God uses to heal His people.

IDENTIFY ACTIONS THAT YOU NEED TO TAKE

Often, healing from a conditioned emotional response requires you to practice behaviors that are opposite from the ones associated with the response. In Kim's case, she found that speaking up in groups and saying when she disagreed with something were important actions she needed to practice. Raymond found that giving a genuine apology rather than justifying his behavior when he acted according to his old pattern was an important key to his healing.

As you consider the behaviors associated with your conditioned emotional response, list several that would be positive and the opposite of what you have done in the past. Then practice doing them whenever the old pattern emerges.

CHAPTER 11

EMOTIONS THAT ARE TABOO

D uring childhood, many people develop defenses against the various physical and emotional threats they experience. In the process, they sometimes learn that certain emotions should never be experienced. As adults, they cover up and flee from these taboo emotions whenever they are triggered. For example, a friend mentions to Jeremy that he must have been disappointed when he lost a large sale. Jeremy immediately makes a joke, laughs, and changes the subject. Later, at home while watching a movie with his wife, a tender moment between the characters occurs. Jeremy, to the annoyance of his wife, automatically begins to talk about work and remembers something that needs his immediate attention.

In this chapter we'll look at how emotions can become taboo along with ways to reconnect with them. We'll also see how they often point to important parts of our lives that need God's healing touch.

WHAT CAUSES AN EMOTION TO BECOME UNACCEPTABLE?

When you look at an infant or a young child, you see a cauldron of emotions. Indeed, one of the primary developmental tasks as we learn to think and reason is how to control our emotions. Sometimes this lesson is learned too well and some emotions become so controlled they recede from conscious awareness.

Some children learn that certain emotions are unacceptable by watching their parents and modeling their behavior. Others grow up in a culture that has strong prohibitions against expressing certain emotions. In some cases, the suppression of certain emotions is necessary for physical or emotional survival. The emotions that most frequently come to be seen as unacceptable fall into three general categories: anger associated with asserting yourself or setting limits; emotions connected with weakness; and emotions connected with intimacy. Let's look at a few examples of the different ways that these types of emotions can become taboo.

Marcella grew up in a country that was devastated by civil unrest. People who spoke up against the government were tortured and killed. To survive, she learned to always be calm and quiet when in public. She learned this both by being told to never show any resistance and by watching what happened to others who did confront the lawless gangs that were prowling about the country. When Marcella finally moved to a country where she was safe, she still found herself behaving as if something bad would happen to her if she spoke up.

Chapter 10 described how Kim was a sensitive child who grew

up with very strict parents. When she became angry, they would respond in an overly aggressive manner that frightened her. Over time Kim learned to suppress her anger to avoid the wrath of her parents. While her parents would never have harmed her, as a young child she felt just as threatened as Marcella.

In chapter 3 you met Ramona who suffered from panic disorder. Ramona's mother learned never to express anger and always to be agreeable as a result of growing up in a violent family. As Ramona grew, she modeled her mother's behavior and learned to suppress anger and please others in the same way her mother did. Their behavior was the same even though Ramona never experienced the trauma that her mother had experienced.

Jeremy, who was introduced at the start of this chapter, grew up in a home where intimacy was not expressed openly. He learned from his father that being a man meant you are always strong and never show weakness. True intimacy involves becoming vulnerable and experiencing the emotions associated with our need for others. To someone who always needs to be strong and in control, these emotions feel like weakness and so must be suppressed whenever they surface.

Kara never knew her father and spent her younger years raised by an emotionally absent mother who was deeply involved with drugs. As with any child, Kara wanted to be close to her mother. However, as her repeated attempts to be close with her mother were rejected or met with indifference, tremendous pain became associated with the need for intimacy and the behaviors related to it. Over time she saw the feelings associated with intimacy, at an unconscious level, as a threat and became anxious whenever they were aroused.

Eventually Kara was removed from her home and spent her remaining childhood in various group homes and foster care families where she received little love. As an adult, she found that intimate situations triggered the intense pain associated with the rejection she received as a child. Whenever she met a man who was comfortable with emotional intimacy, the anxiety associated with intimacy caused her to take actions that would eventually end the relationship. Afterwards, she would wonder why she acted as she did.

THE PROBLEM WITH HIDING FROM YOUR EMOTIONS

In Genesis, we read that when God first created Adam and Eve, "The man and his wife were both naked, and they felt no shame" (Genesis 2:25). If you think about it, this statement is almost shocking. The Old Testament usually views nakedness as shameful and therefore to be avoided. This is especially true of those who are approaching God in worship or other sacred duties. Yet, here in the garden, where God Himself regularly came to meet with Adam and Eve, they were nude but unashamed. Since both the relationships between Adam and Eve as man and wife and between them and their Creator were unclouded by sin, there was no need for them to cover up. There was nothing to hide.

How different things are after the fall. Like Adam and Eve, we often hide our feelings and things we've done from others, from God, and even from ourselves. Each time we do this, we interrupt the healing of whatever it is that we are hiding.

Part of living in a state of grace that is enlivened with the Holy Spirit is learning that there is no longer any need to hide from God. We need to be able to offer up every aspect of our mind and emotions to God, so He can cleanse them and enable them to function as He intended them to function.

In previous chapters you've learned that positive emotions

are usually a response to needs that are being met and negative emotions are usually a response to unmet needs, threats, and loss. When an emotion becomes taboo, it means that you are unable to deal directly with the needs, threats, and losses associated with it. However, because these triggers still exist and demand your attention, you deal with them unconsciously. Unfortunately, when you deal with needs, threats, and losses through unconscious processes, you tend to take actions that are self-defeating and which hurt others, often the people you are closest to.

Looking at the examples in the previous section, Marcella, Kim, and Ramona were often unable to assert themselves effectively and set reasonable limits with others. This meant that important needs were not met. As a result, Marcella often found that she became depressed. Kim would often respond in a passive-aggressive manner towards the person she was unable to confront directly. Ramona became anxious and sometimes experienced a panic attack.

Because Jeremy was not able to deal with weakness consciously, he processed it unconsciously. After losing the important sale, he found himself becoming angry in situations that normally did not bother him. He also found that he said hurtful things to people he cared for.

Kara's difficulty with intimacy led her to activities that offered an intense emotional experience without the need to be truly intimate. She was very active sexually. However, her relationships never lasted long. She also had a good singing voice and found the attention she received when performing to be exhilarating. When neither of these fully satisfied her need for emotional intimacy, she turned to drugs to dull the pain.

HOW TO IDENTIFY TIMES WHEN TABOO EMOTIONS ARE BEING SUPPRESSED

There are two principal ways to avoid experiencing a taboo emotion. The first is to simply cover it with a different, secondary emotion. Because the taboo emotion is a threat, anger and anxiety are the two most commonly experienced secondary emotions.

The second way to avoid feeling an unacceptable emotion is to distract yourself with some activity, as Jeremy did when confronted with a tender moment while watching a movie. Because you are using an automatic and mostly unconscious response to cover up the taboo emotion, the secondary emotions and distracting behaviors used to avoid the taboo emotions are usually inappropriate for the immediate situation, such as Jeremy's humor when faced with a loss.

It usually takes so much mental energy to suppress a taboo emotion that it leaves you little for dealing with your current circumstances. Since the responses associated with a taboo emotion are usually well practiced and partly unconscious, they tend to be fairly robotic in nature.

A good example of this is the way I reacted to embarrassment in my younger years. Soon after getting married, my wife and I moved to Japan where I taught science and math at an international school for two years. As we were beginning to settle in, we would periodically go to the local department store. After being at the store for a short time, I would become irritable and start making critical remarks about whatever my wife was doing. After several trips, she pointed this out to me.

Upon reflection, I realized what was happening: I was embarrassed because I knew only a little Japanese and often was not sure how to respond in a culturally appropriate way. In my family, avoiding mistakes and being right were important. Embarrassment was not acceptable because it indicated that I had made some type of blunder; so I covered up my embarrassment with anger and distracted myself by criticizing my wife. After I identified what was going on, I used the approach in the next section to change the pattern.

Reconnecting with Taboo Emotions

Though it takes time, the process of reconnecting with taboo emotions is a fairly straightforward three-step process. It does require a willingness to experience emotions that are at first uncomfortable, sometimes painfully so. With time however, the discomfort diminishes. As this happens, the process allows you to manage taboo emotions as you would any other emotion. Most important, it frees up all your mental and emotional energy to deal with the situation you are facing in a fully conscious manner. This allows you to choose actions that are more effective and pleasing to God rather than responding in the old self-defeating and automatic manner. It also helps you hear God's voice more clearly, since the guilt, shame, and fear associated with taboo emotions tend to interfere with your relationship with God.

Develop an Emotional Vocabulary
The first step in reconnecting with taboo emotions is learning to identify emotions accurately. People who are uncomfortable with some of their emotions often hide from them by avoiding words that describe true emotions. Here are four general ways in which this is done.

Words that describe your mental state
People often substitute words that describe a mental state in place of words that describe the emotion being experienced.

For example, a person might say, "I feel confused." When you are confused, you don't understand something. This refers to your state of mind. As a result of your confusion you might feel anxious, sad, or angry. However, if you focus on your mental state, you do not have to acknowledge the underlying emotional state. Here are several common examples of words that are used in this way:

Baffled	Confused	Mystified	Puzzled
Bewildered	Confounded	Perplexed	Stumped

Words that describe circumstances
Another way to hide from emotions is to use words that describe circumstances as if they were emotions. For example, a person might say, "I'm feeling frustrated." Frustration describes a circumstance where you are not getting what you want. A person might also say, "I'm feeling helpless." This describes a circumstance where you do not have the power or ability to control events and make them turn out the way you want. This is often due to factors that are beyond your control. Again, these circumstances might cause you to feel angry, sad, or anxious. Here are common examples of words used in this way:

Beaten	Flustered	Helpless	Powerless
Defeated	Foiled	Impotent	Unfulfilled
Defenseless	Frustrated	Let down	Vulnerable

Words that describe personal qualities
A third way to hide from emotions is to substitute words that describe personal qualities for words that describe true emotions. For example, a person might say, "I'm feeling

inadequate." This means that you see yourself as failing to possess some quality or ability that you need to accomplish something. While the following examples are similar to the previous ones, this group of words tends to see circumstances as more the result of personal deficiencies than those before.

Failure	Inadequate	Pitiful	Weak
Hopeless	Inferior	Useless	Worthless

Words that are vague

The fourth way to hide from emotions is to use words that are vague and have a wide range of meaning rather than words that identify specific emotions. For example, a person might say, "That's disturbing." This could mean that the person is experiencing unsettling thoughts or maybe an emotion such as anger, anxiety, or sadness. Here are examples of words used in this manner:

Emotional	Disturbed	Bothered	Distressed
Upset	Unsettled	Troubled	

Since the English language has hundreds of words that describe the various emotions we experience, it is often helpful to start with a fairly short list of words that describe common emotions like the following.

Words that Describe Positive Emotions

Affectionate	Euphoric	Loving	Satisfied
Amused	Excited	Overjoyed	Sentimental
Calm	Exhilarated	Passionate	Serene
Charmed	Glad	Peaceful	Surprised

Cheerful	Gratified	Pleased	Thrilled
Content	Happy	Proud	Tranquil
Delighted	Joyful	Relaxed	Tickled
Elated	Jubilant	Relieved	Wistful
Ecstatic	Lighthearted	Romantic	

Words That Describe Negative Emotions

Afraid	Disgusted	Heartbroken	Morose
Angry	Embarrassed	Horrified	Outraged
Annoyed	Emotionally	Humiliated	Repulsed
Anxious	exhausted	Hurt	Resentful
Ashamed	Envious	In despair	Sad
Bored	Frightened	Incensed	Terrified
Burnt out	Furious	Irritated	
Cold	Grief-stricken	Jealous	
Depressed	Hateful	Melancholy	

For people who are very detached from their emotions, even the above list is too long. In these cases it is often useful to begin with a just the words: *happy, excited, angry, afraid,* and *sad.*

Identify Times when Taboo Emotions Are Active

As mentioned earlier in this chapter, there are two different indicators that can signal when you are suppressing a taboo emotion. The first is a response that covers the taboo emotion with a different, secondary emotion that is out-of-place. Jeremy's laughter and resort to humor when confronted with a disappointing loss is a good example of this. It would be appropriate to be disappointed (a form of sadness), angry, and even fearful if the money from the sale was especially important to meet financial obligations. My own critical remarks when in department stores in Japan are another example. Jeremy's laughter and my irritation were illogical reactions.

Though any emotion can be used to block unwanted feelings or thoughts, the threat posed by the taboo emotion usually triggers anger or anxiety. Take a moment to review your reactions over the past few weeks. Were there any times when you became angry or anxious for no apparent reason? If so, there may be a taboo emotional reaction that you did not want to experience.

The second indicator of the presence of a taboo emotion is a response that seems out of place. Jeremy's tendency to joke about loss or change the subject and become busy whenever anything involving emotional intimacy occurs indicates that, for him, these are taboo experiences.

As you observe your behavior, be aware of times when you escape from a situation by suddenly changing the subject of a conversation or the focus of the activity or even leaving for no apparent reason. You may find a feeling of anxiety accompanies this type of behavior. Keep in mind that the anxiety is usually *not* the taboo emotion but simply a reaction to the threat that the taboo emotion presents.

Practice Experiencing the Taboo Emotion

When you identify a situation where you think you may be experiencing a taboo emotion, think about what was going on just before you experienced the secondary covering emotion or distracted yourself with an out-of-place behavior. Often, you will immediately be aware of the emotion you didn't want to experience. If it does not come up, pretend that you are looking at a movie of yourself and ask, "What does it seem like I am experiencing?" or "What would the average person experience in a situation like this?"

When you identify the taboo emotion, it will replace whatever else you are feeling. It will also probably be uncomfortable; however, after you have done this several times, the discomfort will diminish. If the taboo emotion is associated with emotional wounds from the past, you may also recall childhood events when you experienced this emotion. This gives you the opportunity to look at these events as an adult and deal with emotions that may have been too difficult to deal with as a child.

As you identify the situations that trigger taboo emotions, it becomes easier to identify what is happening in the middle of the experience. At these times do the following:

- Identify the emotion you are experiencing.
- Identify the reason you are experiencing the emotion.
- Remind yourself that this emotion is normal and safe.
- Remind yourself that you can manage your emotions and choose appropriate actions.
- If appropriate, say how you are feeling and why you are feeling that way.

Returning to my experience in Japan, I found that once I identified what was happening, I could take action to change my behavior. Whenever I noticed myself becoming uncomfortable in a department store with my wife, I would mentally say the following:

I am embarrassed because I can't communicate the way I want to and I don't know the customs. It's OK to be embarrassed. While I don't like it, it won't kill me. I don't need to run away from it by attacking my wife.

At first, my embarrassment would last for several minutes. However, after a short time, I found that I would experience a flash of embarrassment that would quickly pass as I acknowledged that I felt like a fish out of water.

Another example of how I used this approach occurred when I first started my counseling practice and began presenting various classes. I would sometimes forget what I wanted to say. At first, I would try to cover up my forgetfulness and found that I would get even further off topic. I soon realized that this was again the result of my feeling embarrassment over making a mistake.

After this discovery, I began handling times like this differently. I would say: "I just forgot what I was going to say; but it will come to me in a minute." I would then go on to something else. I found that two things happened: I no longer felt embarrassed because I wasn't trying to hide anything; and after a minute or two, I would remember what I was going to say.

As you begin to identify situations that trigger taboo emotions, develop a short statement you can say to yourself when you are in a similar situation in the future. In addition, take some time to mentally go back to the situation you are working with. Allow yourself to experience the taboo emotion you avoided. Then mentally rehearse the statement you developed and note how this decreases the intensity of the emotion.

ADDING A SPIRITUAL DIMENSION

As with everything else, taboo emotions have a spiritual side. When you hide from some aspect of yourself that you do not want to experience, it points to an area that God's revelation and the Holy Spirit need to heal. Jeremy's core belief that he should always be strong and in control not only had poisoned his human relationships, but had kept him distant from God. Becoming friendly with the emotions associated with being vulnerable allowed him to address in an *experiential* way the issues he had already identified mentally.

This important point is often lost in the process of healing.

Chapter 2 discussed how essential subjective experience is to true learning. The same is especially true for healing spiritual and emotional wounds. Jeremy had already identified that he was often ridiculed as a child when he made mistakes. He also knew that his chaotic family had caused him to have an excessive need to be in control of his circumstances. It was only when he dealt with the taboo emotions associated with these issues that true change began.

Along with the childhood issues, Jeremy began to realize how difficult it was for him to trust God. As he opened up this area of his life to the Holy Spirit, he found that he was eventually able to have a much closer relationship, not only with others, but also with God.

In my case, my embarrassment was triggered by a need to always have the right answer. As I began to study the Bible and spend more time in prayer and meditation, I found that it was difficult for me to acknowledge my weaknesses. My pride and arrogance needed to be replaced with humility.

The Beatitudes in Matthew 5:3–10 came to have great meaning for me as I prayed for help with this issue. Here at the beginning of His ministry Christ lays out the basic qualities of kingdom people. The first one had special significance for me: "Blessed are the poor in spirit, for theirs is the kingdom of heaven" (verse 3). I learned that the Greek word here for "poor," *ptōchos*, was a word used to describe someone in abject poverty, utter helplessness, and complete destitution who was dependent on others for support.

God showed me that I desperately needed to be "poor" in this sense. I needed to let go of my self-sufficiency and acknowledge my utter spiritual powerlessness and bankruptcy apart from Christ. While I'm much better at remembering my utter dependence on God now than when I first accepted Christ, this is still an issue for me.

Whenever you identify a taboo emotion, realize that it often signals that there are hurts from the past or traits in your character that need to be healed. It is likely that such hurts or character traits also interfere with your relationship with God. Take time to pray and ask God to show you the spiritual issue that this taboo emotion is pointing to that needs His healing touch. When you do identify an issue, find verses that address it and spend time studying and reflecting on them.

In closing this chapter, I would also like to remind you that deep wounds from the past often take a long time to heal. After all, in some cases you've been avoiding them for years. You will probably find that their effects will continue to resurface now and then — most often when you are sick, hungry, tired, hurt, or stressed due to a difficult life event. At these times, return to measures you took when you first addressed the issue. Lean on people you trust, and take counsel with them. Most important, spend extra time in prayer seeking strength and guidance from the Master Physician.

Suggestions for when Disturbing Memories Surface

This chapter mentioned that a taboo emotion often arises from childhood events which made the emotions dangerous or unacceptable. Because the events associated with taboo emotions are painful, they are also often suppressed. Because of this, it is a common experience to recall painful childhood events when taboo emotions are first experienced consciously. As you take time to reexperience these childhood events and emotions and reinterpret them from an adult perspective, they cease to be a threat. Once you have done this, the taboo emotions will be triggered less often by present situations that resemble the past in some way.

If this seems too overwhelming because you experienced severe abuse or trauma, seek help. However, many people find the following guidelines work well for the typical types of painful events we all experienced as children.

Give yourself time to explore painful memories that surface

When dealing with painful memories from childhood, you need to give yourself time and privacy so you can work through them fully. If you are in a situation, such as at work, where you are unable to explore the memory that surfaced, tell yourself a statement such as the following:

> *This is just a memory from the past. I am an adult now. It cannot harm me or control me. I will deal with it later. Right now I need to focus on the task at hand.*

After this reminder to yourself, find something to do that will distract you from the memory and the emotions associated with it. Be sure to then revisit this memory later when you have time to work through it. Do not continue to ignore and suppress a memory that continues to resurface. If it is surfacing, it is time to deal with it. If you don't, it will continue to resurface and cause problems, usually at inconvenient times. It is wiser to deal with it at a time and place of your choosing.

Remind yourself of three truths about painful childhood events.

As you recall the memory, remind yourself of the following three truths:

- This event is in the past. It is no longer part of the present.
- These circumstances will never happen again. Be

specific as to why this is true. For example, it may be that the people involved in the experience are dead or no longer part of your life.

- Things are different now. You are now an adult and have choices along with the ability to protect yourself that you didn't have as a child. Be specific: "As an adult I can say 'no'," "I can walk away," or "I can get help and protect myself."

Reinterpret the memory from an adult perspective

The beliefs and thoughts associated with painful childhood memories were those of a child. Ask yourself, "How does Jesus see this event?" Then remind yourself of this answer as you again consider the events that you remember. If you are dealing with very painful memories, it is often helpful to write out a statement about the events you recalled. Here is an example of a statement Kara developed in response to memories she had of being left alone.

> *I used to think that I was left alone because there was something wrong with me—that I was unlovable. This is a lie. I was left alone because my mom was a drug addict who was unable to care for a child. This is not what God wanted. God's plan was to have loving parents love and protect their children. Because I live in a broken world where there is evil, I was mistreated as a child. It was never my fault. God loves me. He showed it by sending Jesus to die for me (John 3:16). He shows it now by bringing people into my life who love me. Praise God that He is helping me see the tremendous love that He has for me and the tremendous value that He places on me (1 John 3:1; Romans 8:38–39).*

YOU DON'T NEED TO DO THIS ON YOUR OWN

If at any time you encounter emotions or memories that seem overwhelming seek help. Find people God can use to help carry your burden (Galatians 6:2) and assist you in your healing. Guidelines for finding a counselor are provided in Appendix 3: Suggestions for Seeking Help.

▶RECOMMENDED ACTIVITIES

USE ACCURATE LANGUAGE WHEN TALKING OR THINKING ABOUT CIRCUMSTANCES AND EVENTS

This chapter discusses four ways people avoid words that describe emotions by substituting words that describe mental states, circumstances, or personal qualities—or by simply being vague. The words listed in the examples can be appropriate if they are used correctly. Here are some guidelines for doing this.

Words that describe your mental state
Most of the words listed in the chapter for this category describe some degree of confusion. For the person who needs to be in control or always right, this can be difficult to admit. However, we all regularly encounter situations that we don't understand. When this happens, say so directly. Here are some examples:

Instead of saying	Say
I'm feeling bewildered.	I'm bewildered by this. *OR* I'm bewildered.

Instead of saying (con't)	Say (con't)
I'm feeling confused.	I'm confused by this. OR This confuses me.
I'm feeling stumped.	I'm stumped by this.

Words that describe circumstances

Most of the words listed in the chapter for this category describe circumstances where you lack the ability to accomplish what you want or where you have failed at some task. Again, this is a normal part of life. There is no shame in admitting this. Instead, it helps you lean on God more and allows Him to help you do what you cannot do by yourself. Here are examples of how you could use the words on this list more accurately:

Instead of saying	Say
I'm feeling frustrated.	I'm frustrated. OR This frustrates me.
I'm feeling helpless about this.	I'm helpless to do anything about his. OR I can't do anything about this.
I'm feeling powerless about this.	I'm powerless to do anything about this.

Words that describe personal qualities

The words listed in the chapter for this category are often used to describe one's entire being in a negative light. This is especially true for people with a poor self-image where these words are a reflection of their core beliefs. Thus, "I'm feeling like a failure," often means, "I am a failure."

If you are going to use these words, it is important not to use them as a general label for who you are. Instead, limit them to a specific event or circumstance. Often, it is best to substitute a more positive word. Here are examples that show both types of substitutions:

Instead of saying	Say
I'm feeling like a failure.	I failed at that task. *OR* I didn't do what I wanted with this.
I'm feeling hopeless.	This situation is hopeless. *OR* This situation doesn't seem like it's going to work out.
I'm feeling inadequate.	I can't do this. *OR* I can't do this as I would like to do it.

Words that are vague

Generally, it is best to avoid vague words like the ones listed in the chapter. The big exception is when you are in a situation where it would not be appropriate to reveal too much about yourself. This includes social events where people simply are not interested in all the details of your life. It also includes situations where you are dealing with people who are not trustworthy or safe.

Did any of the suggested phrases make you uncomfortable as you read through them? If so, your discomfort probably means that it is something you need to practice. You may be aware of why it made you uncomfortable. If not, ask God to help you see why you reacted the way you did. Once you have identified the reason for your reaction, review the list of destructive core beliefs in Chapter 6. Identify any that might be contributing to your reaction.

PRACTICE IDENTIFYING EMOTIONS ACCURATELY

Review the lists of words that describe positive and negative emotions once each day this week. Practice using them when talking to others and when you are doing the exercises in this book.

Whenever you are upset, take a moment to identify the emotion you are experiencing. Once you have identified the emotion, identify the need or want that is generating it and decide on the most appropriate course of action. Keep in mind that if you are sick, hungry, tired, hurt, or stressed it is often wise to wait before taking action. Continue to practice identifying emotions until it is easy to do.

IDENTIFY TABOO EMOTIONS THAT MAY BE INTERFERING WITH YOUR LIFE

Take some time to reflect on your behavior over the past few weeks and identify any times when you experienced inappropriate emotions or acted in a way that was inappropriate for the situation. If you identify any, take some time to identify the underlying taboo emotion along with why this emotional reaction has become taboo. Here are several questions you can ask yourself:

- Did either of my parents react like this?
- How did my parents react when I displayed this emotion?
- What was I told about this type of emotion?
- Are there events in my past that have caused me not to want to experience this?
- What do I believe about this type of emotion?

After you have identified why this emotion is taboo, develop a short statement similar to the examples in the chapter that you can use to help you reconnect with this emotion. Also be sure to identify the spiritual issue that this taboo emotion points to. If this is difficult, ask God to open your eyes to what you need to learn and where you need to grow. Once you identify the spiritual issue, take time to ask God to heal this area of your life. You may need to talk to someone about it. It will also help to find Bible passages that relate to it. Here are several common issues that can be associated with taboo emotions:

Abandonment	Losing power or	Safety
Danger	social position	Sex
Disapproval	Making mistakes	Success
Failure	Personal worth	Uncertainty
Intimacy	Pleasure	
Lack of control	Rejection	

As mentioned previously, if the issues you identify seem overwhelming, find someone to help you. Guidelines for finding a counselor are provided in Appendix 3: Suggestions for Seeking Help.

Reinterpret Painful Memories that Are Triggered by Taboo Emotions

This chapter mentioned that taboo emotions are often associated with childhood events where you experienced this emotion. It also provided guidelines for working through these types of painful memories so they no longer act as emotional triggers. Take time to do this whenever a painful memory surfaces. If you need to focus on the present circumstances, work through the memory later when you are alone and have time.

CHAPTER 12

TRUE EMOTIONAL HEALING

I n the first chapter of Genesis we learn that after God created people, He commanded them, "Be fruitful and increase in number; fill the earth and subdue it" (Genesis 1:28). Science has played an important role in the process of "subduing" the earth as attested by the many marvels of modern science and the fact that our lives are far more comfortable than those of our ancestors. However, in our modern technological world, it's easy to forget that what we see is not all that there is.

Just as we are surrounded by radio and television signals that we cannot see, we are part of an invisible spiritual world that surrounds us and interacts with us daily. As Paul states, "Our struggle is not against flesh and blood, but against the rulers, against the authorities, against the powers of this dark world and against the spiritual forces of evil in the heavenly realms" (Ephesians 6:12). So, while modern medicine and psychology have found many ways to help people, something is always missing when we rely on human wisdom and science alone to solve our problems.

God provided a vivid illustration of this to me recently. During a Bible study my friend Warren described some of his experiences with a therapist who was working with a nine-year-old boy he was adopting. This boy had been in therapy for a year due to intense anger. He'd had a rough life during his first eight years, and his anger was being expressed in severe behavioral problems. As Warren began working with him as a foster parent, he took a role in the boy's therapy. During the Bible study, Warren spoke of experiencing the difference between an approach based solely on human wisdom and effort and one that was based on a biblical view of God and guided by the Holy Spirit.

Warren described the therapist as warm, caring, and well trained. However, she saw God as simply a word that stood for the good in the world. As a result, she made statements such as, "There is good in everybody, therefore God is in everybody. He is all around. He is nature." As Warren worked with the boy, he not only provided the warm, loving home that many foster parents do, but he also used Scripture and prayer to help the youngster see himself and others as Jesus saw him. The transformation was amazing.

Warren recalled a particular conversation where the therapist expressed how she was dumbfounded at the profound changes this child had made since coming to live with him. She asked Warren to share what he was doing differently from her other clients. He said, "We simply live our lives according to the Word of God—not just hearing it, but doing it and living in it." As usually happens with those who do not know the healing power of God, it was impossible for her to understand how that could be true. The answer seemed too simple.

What is often not understood in both medicine and counseling is that a complete healing requires the healing of not only the body and mind but also the spirit and soul. This is what Warren's therapist could not grasp. Indeed, it is impossible for someone who has not been reborn to understand God's healing power. As Paul states, "The man without the Spirit does not accept the things that come from the Spirit of God, for they are foolishness to him, and he cannot understand them, because they are spiritually discerned" (1 Corinthians 2:14).

All the struggles we face have a spiritual dimension. As discussed in previous chapters, our struggles reveal our current level of maturity and provide opportunities for personal spiritual growth as well as the opportunity to advance God's plan for creation. Addressing the spiritual aspect is often the key to resolving or — in chronic cases — effectively managing many physical, mental, and emotional problems. Unfortunately, we often deal with our struggles without considering their spiritual dimensions.

When I began my counseling career, I had been away from the church since childhood and worked from a purely secular perspective. After a few years, I started attending a local church, renewed my commitment to Christ, and began to integrate a biblical perspective into my counseling. I also started to hear testimonies of how the Holy Spirit healed the damaged emotions of people without the use of psychiatric medications and psychological techniques.

Please don't misunderstand what I've just said. I did not abandon all that I had learned. I find that there is much in modern psychiatric medicines and psychology that is a great benefit to people. My point is that all true healing comes from God through the Holy Spirit. Modern medications and psychological techniques can play an important role in the healing of damaged emotions. However, the healing of the inner spirit and soul requires more than just a healing of the body or a change in one's beliefs. Spiritual issues such as a petrifying fear of death, an ever-present shame, an unforgiving heart that carries deep resentments over past hurts or abusive relationships, or an anger over the fact that life is not going according to our plan can only be truly resolved with God's help. Any physical or psychological healing will fall short of the true healing that God wants for us unless it addresses our sin nature and God's desire for us to be transformed into the image of Christ.

Over the years I've worked with many people in both private practice and in church-sponsored self-help groups. In both settings, and in the testimonies of friends at church, I've witnessed God heal a range of difficult problems from substance abuse and anxiety disorders to lives crippled by shame, anger, guilt, and resentment. Sometimes this occurred with the aid of counseling. Sometimes medications played a role. God uses a variety of means to reach out to and heal His people; however, the key elements for those who were truly healed were always the combination of a sincere commitment to Christ, personal prayer time, Bible study, and active participation in a loving, Christ-centered church. Here are two examples from friends of mine, J.W. and Cricket, in their own words. Each shows what the Holy Spirit can do.

J.W.

My father was a very abusive man. Small things would set him off. He would have anger fits where he would beat my mother or us kids for what we did. After he did this he would disappear for several days and then return home like nothing ever happened. He never discussed these outbreaks with us and years later denied they ever happened.

When I made the decision to accept Christ into my life, one of the issues God had me work on was the relationship with my father. I did not speak to him and returned any Christmas and birthday gifts he would send. While the forgiveness within me was a journey in and of itself, it has made me a better person for it. In forgiving my father for all the sins he committed against me, I learned to forgive myself and accept the grace that God has to offer through Christ. The hatred and the anger were a bag of bricks that I gave to God and walked away from. I was blessed with a wonderful relationship with my father during the last ten years of his life, and I realize what a great gift God has given me through forgiveness and love. In leaving the bitterness and the turmoil behind me, I gained greater peace as well as deeper relationships with my wife and children. God has made me a better person through the teaching of forgiveness.

Cricket

When I was born, my mother didn't want me and had nothing to do with me. Because my father was dying I received little care. Eventually my mother abandoned me, my sister, and brother. My father did what he could until he died when I was two years old.

The three of us made the rounds in the Sacramento County system. This was a very difficult time as my brother and sister would be taken from the orphanage, and I would be left behind. The seed of rejection started very early for me. My grandmother took custody of all of us a year or so later. We lived with her until I was seven years old.

Then, we were reinstated with my mother, a step-father and three other children. Throughout my childhood my mother made it clear she did not like me. While there was no physical abuse, the constant verbal abuse made it difficult for me to like myself, and trusting anyone became a real issue for me.

At eighteen I moved out and made my way into the adult

world. I had attended church a little bit as a child with my grandmother and at times with friends to get out of my house. As an adult, I started going to church with my boyfriend. After we broke up, I stopped going.

When I was about to be married, I wanted a "real pastor" to marry us so we began searching for one. We were invited to attend the church where I still attend. We met the pastor and during a visit he asked a question that no one had ever asked me: "Have you accepted Jesus into your heart?" That night I did and my world changed dramatically.

In 1978 I became pregnant with my first child. During my pregnancy I stayed home and spent most of my days studying the Bible. Little did I know that it was going to prepare me for what I was about to face. My son was born with multiple disabilities, and my world was turned upside down. Prayer was my mainstay, and my church family was my total support system. My mother totally rejected my son just as she had me. It was very hurtful and painful.

Many years passed, and I struggled and worked hard at finding the peace that only the Holy Spirit could provide me. By continually seeking out God in prayer and the counsel of mature Christian friends and Bible study, the peace and healing I needed came. I learned to love unconditionally. I learned to love myself so I could love others. I learned how to forgive and give to the Lord those things in my life that pained me.

Before I came to know the Lord, I was a very bitter, angry, and confused person who didn't trust ANYONE. After I accepted the Lord and made Him a daily part of my life and began studying who He is and how He desires me to live, my life began changing. It didn't happen overnight. It has been a journey but a journey that I have never regretted. My life has not been an easy one, but it has been filled with adventures that are amazing.

Only God and the Holy Spirit can take the garbage in one's life and turn it into a decadent feast. The first two Bible verses I memorized when I first accepted the Lord were "Seek ye first the kingdom of God, and His righteousness; and all these things shall be added unto you" (Matthew 6:33) and "We know that all things work together for good to those who love God, to those who are called according to His purpose" (Romans 8:28). These are two Scriptures that have been my mainstay through all the challenges through the years. Staying in God's Word daily and having a church family, regular attendance at church, and having a regular time of prayer have brought healing that would never have happened for me in any other way.

When looking at emotional problems, keep in mind that the goal is not merely relief from the personal pain they cause or the problems they create in daily life and relationships. The goal is to become more like Christ. The healing that you receive is a blessing that is meant to glorify God and bless others. In the process you will find a healing that is much deeper and richer than you would have thought possible.

"No eye has seen, no ear has heard, no mind has conceived what God has prepared for those who love him" (1 Corinthians 2:9).

Six Steps for Managing Emotions Effectively

Before closing, I would like to give some general guidelines for managing difficult emotions in a way that glorifies God. These guidelines are meant for times when you experience emotions that seem overwhelming or puzzling or when you have responded to a situation in an ungodly or self-defeating way. Be sure to ask God to open your heart and mind to His guidance before you begin.

Step 1: What Am I Feeling?

Clearly identify what emotion you experienced. Be sure to use words that describe true emotions as discussed in chapter 11. If you are working with an inappropriate behavior, identify what you were feeling just before you reacted. If this is difficult for you, take some time to review chapter 11 which addresses this issue in detail.

Step 2: What Triggered this Emotion?

Chapter 5 describes how most emotions are a response to needs and wants being met, a perceived threat, or a loss that has been experienced. Once you identify what you felt, the easiest way to identify the need or want that triggered it is to ask yourself, "What did I want in this situation?" or "If I could control events, what should have happened?" As you describe what you would have liked to happen, identify the specific need or want that was frustrated or the loss that occurred.

Step 3: Was My Emotional Response Appropriate?

When answering this question, first decide if the response was a logical response. If there was a real threat, then some level of anger or fear would be appropriate. If a loss occurred, sadness would be appropriate.

Next, ask yourself if the level of the emotion fit the situation. If the emotion was logical and at an appropriate level of intensity, go on to the next step. If not, ask yourself the following questions:

- Were there any hidden needs generating this emotion, such as the need for others to like me, the need to control others or events, the need to be right, or the desire for revenge?

- Did my thinking involve any of the unbiblical forms of thinking described in chapter 5?
- Did negative core beliefs such as those described in chapter 6 play a role?
- Was this a conditioned emotional response as described in chapter 10?
- Was this emotion simply covering a taboo emotion as described in chapter 11? If so, what was the taboo emotion?

Step 4: Were the Actions I Took Appropriate?

Most of the time, simply asking yourself the question, "Was my behavior something that glorified God?" is enough. However, if you are not sure, talk to someone who is mature in the Lord. This might be a fellow believer or a pastor. An objective third person is often helpful in looking at your behavior more clearly.

Step 5: What Does God Want Me to Learn from This?

Because we are experts at rationalizing our responses, this is often the most difficult step. However, if you ask God with a sincere heart to help you see what He wants you to learn from this experience, He will reveal it to you. Unfortunately, we often don't like the answer and refuse to listen. Be willing to allow God to lead you to those things in your life that are keeping you distant from Him and need His healing touch. These often involve fear, pride, resentment, self-importance, emotional wounds, or sin that you are reluctant to give up.

Step 6: Is There Some Action I Need to Take?

Strong emotions always indicate a need to take action. Sometimes the action involves dealing with unresolved hurts from the past, ungodly beliefs, pride, or sin in your life. This is especially true if you identified issues like this in Steps 3 or 5. Other times, your emotions are signaling that you need to take another type of action. If you have clearly identified a need or want that is reasonable and doesn't violate what has been revealed in Scripture, ask God to help you plan actions that will please Him.

Sometimes the required action has to do with setting limits or confronting someone. Sometimes it involves making changes in your life or pursuing something your heart desires that you have been ignoring. If it is difficult for you to identify actions you can take that would be appropriate and pleasing to God, seek the counsel of other believers or your minister.

►Recommended Activities

Practice the Six Steps for Managing Emotions Effectively

During this week, practice going through the six steps outlined in this chapter. You can work through an incident you have recorded previously, or you can apply them to a situation you encounter during the week. Keep in mind that they are meant for situations where you experience emotions that seem overwhelming or puzzling or when you have responded to a situation in an ungodly or self-defeating way.

Plan to Review

It is impossible to get everything out of a book like this in one reading. I encourage you to go back through it a second time. Spend extra time with those sections and exercises which you feel are especially important to you. If you have read the book on your own, consider forming a small group to work through it. Questions that can be used to stimulate discussion in a small group are located at the end of the book. Many find that hearing others discuss the ideas that have been presented greatly increases their understanding and helps them apply them more effectively.

A Question for You

In Cricket's testimonial, she told of how in spite of having gone to church as a child and then as an adult, no one had asked her, "Have you accepted Jesus into your heart?" If you have never accepted Jesus as your Lord and Savior, I would ask that you consider doing so now by:

- Acknowledging that you are a sinner and in need of Savior — this is usually called repenting and turning away from sin
- Believing in your heart that God raised Jesus from the dead after he paid the full penalty for your sins
- Surrendering control of your life to Jesus — this is often referred to as confessing Jesus as your Lord and Savior

If you are not sure how to do this, here is a suggested prayer:

Father God, I have broken your laws and my sins have separated me from you. I am truly sorry, and now I want to turn away from my past sinful life. Please forgive me. I believe that Your Son, Jesus Christ died for my sins, was resurrected from the dead, is alive, and hears my prayer. I now ask Jesus to come into my life and take control of every aspect of it. I place my trust in You alone for my salvation, and I accept your free gift of eternal life.

If you have just accepted Christ as your Lord and Savior, the next step is to be baptized as a public declaration of your faith. Talk to someone you know who is a committed Christian or to a pastor about this. It is also time to begin studying the Bible and fellowshipping at a church so you can learn what it means to be a Christian. If you are not attending a church, look at Appendix 1: Suggestions on How to Find a Good Church.

SUGGESTIONS ON HOW TO FIND A GOOD CHURCH

While there are probably many different churches in your area, keep in mind that you are looking for more than just a building and a good sermon. You are looking for a fellowship of believers who reflect the body of Christ. This is the true church: people who love the Lord and love each other. Here you find people who will love you and to whom you can give your love. You will also find opportunities to serve and grow spiritually.

First Step

Proverb 3:5–6 says, "Trust in the LORD with all your heart and lean not on your own understanding; in all your ways acknowledge him, and he will make your paths straight." God knows both you and the churches in your area. Ask Him to guide you to the one that is best for you and to give you wisdom so you will recognize the church home that will be best for you. Do this regularly until you find the church that He wants you to join.

Where to Look

A good place to start is with Christian friends and relatives. Ask where they worship and what they like and dislike about the church they attend. You might also ask if they have been to any other churches in your vicinity and what they know about them. If you are new to an area or don't know anyone who attends church regularly, look through your local paper or telephone book. You can also search via the Internet. Most churches now have websites that can give you some idea of what they are like. You can also note churches in your neighborhood as you drive around.

It is best if you can find a church that is nearby. Attending a church that is far from where you live often becomes an excuse for being absent. When your church is close, it's easier to attend small group meetings as well as mid-week activities. At the same time, it is sometimes worth it to travel a little farther to belong to a church that provides a spiritually rich and loving environment in which to grow.

Things to Look For

As you evaluate a church, keep in mind: it will not be perfect. Any church is made up of a group of people who have all the short-comings you find in any group. Each church also has its own feel and personality. Don't expect it to match one you have known in the past. However, good churches do share the following characteristics.

The Bible Is the Basis of Its Teaching

Jesus said, "My mother and brothers are those who hear God's word and put it into practice" (Luke 8:21). In the parable of the wise and foolish builders, He said that the man who "hears my words and puts them into practice" is like the wise builder who laid a deep foundation on rock so it could withstand the flood when it struck (Luke 6:46–49).

A good church bases its teaching on the Bible and lifts up Jesus Christ in all its activities. The sermons deepen your understanding of the Word of God. They do not simply entertain but challenge you to move out of your comfort zone and become more of what God intended you to be: the image of Christ.

Avoid churches that focus on psychology, politics, or sources other than the Bible for their teaching. While this is usually clear from simply observing a few sermons, most churches will also provide a printed statement of their beliefs if you ask for it. You might also ask about the church's history and government.

Spirit-Filled Worship

While talking to the Samaritan woman, Jesus said, "A time is coming and has now come when the true worshipers will worship the Father in spirit and truth, for they are the kind of worshipers the Father seeks. God is spirit, and his worshipers must worship in spirit and in truth" (John 4:23–24). During worship, check to see whether those gathered are merely going through the motions or are genuinely worshiping and adoring God.

An Atmosphere of Love, Joy, and Unity among the Members

Jesus said, "By this all men will know that you are my disciples, if you love one another" (John 13:35). One way you can tell that the Holy Spirit is alive and active in a congregation is through the love and friendship its members have for one another. You should feel welcomed and see genuine fellowship among the members.

Opportunities to Grow in Christ

In one of Jesus' teachings, he compared himself to a vine and God to a gardener to emphasize the need to stay closely connected to Him. He then said, "This is to my Father's glory, that you bear much fruit, showing yourselves to be my disciples" (John 15:8). A little later He emphasized, "I chose you and appointed you to go and bear fruit—fruit that will last" (verse 15:16).

Look at the church bulletin to see if there are small groups you can become involved in to deepen your understanding of the Bible and provide a place for spiritual growth. Being a member of a small group is how you form deep relationships with others and discover in an experiential way, the deeper truths of the gospel.

If you have children, see whether the children's and youth program is mainly there to entertain, or whether it gives solid biblical teaching. Strong youth programs also give the youth of the church ways to serve and participate in mission activities.

Opportunities for Service and an Active Missions Program

After washing the disciples' feet, Jesus said, "I have set you an example that you should do as I have done for you" (see John 13:12–17). Churches where Christ is alive show it through a heart for missions as well as programs that both reach out to and serve their surrounding community.

How to Proceed

Once you have identified a church that might be a good fit, attend several worship services to get a general feel for the church. Before going, ask God to give you wisdom in evaluating the church. Be sure to look through the bulletin to see what types of groups and activities the church offers. Ask if there is a brochure that describes the church's beliefs and background. Talk to members and ask them what they like about the church and what they don't like.

Sometimes, you know right away that a church is not for you. However, if you are not sure, attend for a month before making up your mind. It is often difficult to evaluate a church after attending only one service. You may have attended on a Sunday when there was a guest pastor, a missionary speaker, or some other special service that does not give you a full picture of what the church is like. After several visits, if you are thinking about joining the church, have a meeting with the pastor away from the worship service. Ask about the pastor's background, beliefs, and vision for the church. You do not want to blindly follow someone you don't know.

Do not rush into joining a church. You are looking for a family that loves and accepts you. Of course, you also need to love and accept them. So spend time fellowshipping with church members and getting to know the church before you make a decision.

SUGGESTIONS ON HOW TO DEVELOP A REGULAR PRAYER LIFE

P rayer is simply talking to God, something you can do while driving, working, relaxing at home, or any other time. God wants you to be so comfortable that you talk to Him throughout the day. This is the essence of relationship with God.

In addition to these informal conversations with God, it is also good to have a regular time set apart from your day, away from the world's interruptions, to commune with God. Jesus did this regularly. In fact, you find many examples in the Gospels of Jesus withdrawing from the crowds to be alone and pray.

Learning to develop the habit of regular private prayer is similar to starting an exercise routine. When undertaking an exercise routine, at first it is wise to only do a little. Then, as the muscles develop, you can exercise more strenuously and for longer periods. In the same way, start with a short, regular prayer time of five to ten minutes. As you begin to reap the benefits of regular time alone with God, you will probably want to spend longer in prayer.

While there are many ways to spend your time with God, the following ideas offer a good place to start.

Choose a time and place.

Decide on a time and place where you will not be disturbed. Many like to pray at the start of their day. However, if you are not a morning person, choose a time during the day or in the evening when your mind is clear.

Prepare your heart and mind.

The most common way that people shift their attention from the world to God is to begin their prayer time with a short reading from either the Bible or a good devotional. If you are not sure what to read, ask your pastor or a mature Christian friend for help. There are many excellent devotionals and Bible reading plans available both in book form and on the Internet. You can even have daily devotions sent to you via e-mail. Some find that beginning their time of prayer by listening to worship music or singing helps prepare their hearts for submission.

Recall blessings you've received.

People often see prayer as simply a time to present God with a list of things they want. This is not how you would approach someone you love. Instead, take a moment to reflect on the past day or so, thank God for the good things that have occurred, and praise Him. People who only view God as a cosmic Santa Claus do not learn the importance of being thankful and reflecting on how God cares for us in our daily lives.

Reflect on your shortcomings, and confess your sins.
Identify times during the past day when you have acted in an unloving way towards others along with any anger or resentment to which you are clinging. Confess these to God, and ask for His help in responding in these situations as He wants you to respond. Keep in mind that this is not a salvation issue. Once you accept Christ as your Savior, you are saved. However, sin distances you from God.

Asking for forgiveness humbles us and draws us closer to God. This is why James, when talking about the need to submit to God, quotes Proverbs 3:34, "God opposes the proud but gives grace to the humble" (James 4:6). He then says, "Come near to God and he will come near to you" (verse 8). These are both common themes in the Old and New Testaments.

As you confess your sins and shortcomings, be aware of thoughts that God might be giving you as to actions you need to take. The more you practice this, the more easily you will hear His leading.

Present your petitions to God.
You are now ready to bring your petitions to God. As you make your requests, consider what God wants you to learn through each experience or situation you bring before Him. Be sure to also ask for guidance in how to best be His agent in the troubling circumstances you are facing.

As you practice praying, you will find that you may often depart from these guidelines. That is fine. As you grow in prayer, you will find many other ways to be with God. For example, you might just spend a few moments in silence after any of these phases of your prayer time. Being silent allows God to bring thoughts to your mind that you might otherwise be too busy to hear. This is one important way in which God speaks to us. For example, silence after reading the Bible passage or devotional can allow you to see deeper truths in the text. Silence after thanksgiving can deepen your appreciation of God's love. Silence after petitions can bring a deeper understanding of how God is using painful circumstances to form you into the person He wants you to be.

Another way to learn how to pray more effectively is to spend time praying with others. Become part of a prayer group at your church where you can pray with people who have a rich prayer life. There are many great examples of prayer in the Bible such as the Lord's Prayer in Matthew 6: 9–13. Paul often opened or closed his letters with excellent examples of prayer. Additional examples of prayers by Paul can be found scattered throughout his writings. Reading one of these at the start of your prayer time is a great way to begin. The Psalms can also provide a rich source of material to begin your time of prayer.

SUGGESTIONS FOR SEEKING HELP

The first question to consider when seeking counsel for emotional problems is "What kind of help do I want?" This may sound somewhat simplistic at first, but there are many different types of aid available. For example, many find that self-help groups provide all the assistance they need; others find individual counseling is needed. Within each of these two general types, you find groups and counselors that use a purely secular approach and those that offer a rich spiritual component grounded in a solid biblical foundation.

Three main things set Christian self-help groups and counselors apart from secular ones:

- The leaders of the group or the individuals doing the counseling are Christian.

- Christ is at the center of everything that is done.
- Everything that is done is consistent with biblical principles.

One problem when seeking assistance is the reality that in some areas Christian resources are hard to find. This is not necessarily a problem. Just as a broken leg can be set by a non-Christian physician, some emotional problems have major physical or mental aspects that can be addressed effectively by non-Christian groups and counselors.

When receiving help from non-Christian sources, keep in mind that the spiritual aspects of your problem, as discussed in this book, are not being addressed. Finding ways to address them through pastoral counseling or a church based group may be the key to a full healing. Also be aware that secular self-help groups and counselors often have a worldview that is very different from the Bible. This is not necessarily a problem as long as you are aware of it. However, in some cases it can be counterproductive when the group or individual counselor is hostile to Christianity and biblical ideas.

Among self-help groups, there are national Christian-based groups such as Celebrate Recovery as well as local church-sponsored groups and programs such as divorce recovery workshops. There are also many secular groups like Alcoholics Anonymous and self-help groups sponsored by mental health organizations. Many major emotional problems have national self-help organizations that can provide good resources such as the Obsessive-Compulsive Foundation and the Depression and Bipolar Support Alliance.

Using the Internet to Locate Resources

When looking for self-help or educational groups in your area, begin with a simple search of the Internet. Enter the type of problem you are facing such as "panic disorder" or "depression"; then add your city. Here is an example of what I would enter into a search engine if I were looking for local resources on panic disorder in my area:

"panic disorder" Sacramento CA

Note that the quotation marks tells the search engine to first look for "panic disorder." The name of my city outside the quotation marks then narrows the search to those entries that also have the words Sacramento and CA. If I wanted to search for national organizations that deal with panic disorder, I would enter:

"panic disorder" national organization

Locating Individual Counselors

Within the area of individual counseling there are five general types of help available:

Pastoral counselors – These can be ministers, priests, or lay counselors connected to a church. Some have extensive training in counseling while others do not.

Psychiatrists – These are medical doctors who specialize in treating conditions that have a biological component such as biological depression and obsessive compulsive disorder. Because they are doctors (MDs), they can prescribe medication.

Psychologists – These individuals usually have a doctorate (PhD) in psychology.

Marriage and family therapists – These individuals usually
have a master's degree (M.A. or M.S.), or sometimes a
doctorate (PhD), in counseling or psychology.

Social workers – Social workers who conduct individual
therapy are often referred to as clinical social workers.
They usually have a master's degree (MA or MS), or
sometimes a doctorate (PhD), in social work.

Here are a set of questions you can ask when seeking help from
an individual counselor:

Are you a Christian? If yes, what role does Christianity play
in your counseling?

- Do you pray with clients?
- Do you use Scripture as part of your counseling?

If no, how do you feel about working with Christians? Do
you have any religious or spiritual beliefs? If so, what are
they?

What training and experience do you have with my type of
problem?

What type of approach do you take with my type of problem?

What do you charge and is any of it covered by insurance?

How often will we meet?

How many sessions do you think it will take to resolve this
issue?

After going to a self-help group or meeting with an individual counselor two or three times, ask yourself the following
questions:

Am I comfortable with this person/group?

Is it safe to say whatever I want?

Do I leave meetings with the feeling that something positive
has taken place?

Does the approach make sense to me and seem relevant to my
problem?

Has a plan of action been developed with clear goals?

When I pray about counseling sessions or things that have
taken place in the group, am I reassured that I am in the
right place?

If you answer no to any of these questions, seriously reconsider
whether the group or individual is the right one for you.

Both in seeking help and evaluating the help you are receiving,
it often helps to discuss things with your pastor, a church elder,
or a mature Christian friend you trust. At the same time, God
gave you a mind and the ability to evaluate people and events. He
expects you to use them whenever you seek help. Always take time
to pray about a meeting or session you have attended. Consider
the things you have been told and asked to do to make sure that
they align with the truths that the Bible teaches and that they fit
your needs and circumstances. Make sure you ask God to give you
wisdom as you do this.

It's OK to stop working with someone if you believe that no
progress is being made or that the work is counterproductive. Do
not be afraid to speak up and discuss your concerns about slow
progress or lack of progress with your counselor. If the counselor
reacts negatively, this is an important indication that he or she may
not be the right person to work with.

SMALL GROUP DISCUSSION QUESTIONS

GETTING READY

You are about to take a journey together. During this first session it is important to get to know one another and set a direction for you personally as well as for the group.

- If there are members of the group who do not know everyone, it is recommended that everyone have name tags for the first three meetings.
- Everyone should have their own copy of the book by the start of the first meeting. If books are going to be purchased in bulk, they can be distributed during the first meeting.
- Make a group decision as to whether there will be snacks. If so, how will they be provided?
- Decide whether one person will lead each meeting or whether leadership will be rotated. If it is to be rotated, how will this be done?

- A common format for many small groups that are meeting outside of church is:
  - Study
  - Prayer
  - Fellowship/Refreshments
- If you are meeting at church on Sunday during the adult Bible study hour, a discussion followed by a short time of prayer is common.

As you go through the discussion questions for each chapter, do not feel as though you need to complete every question. They are simply meant to be a starting point. Sometimes groups find that a thorough discussion of a few questions is more beneficial than completing them all. There also may be times when a chapter generates a valuable discussion that is not related to the questions. Be willing to go where the Holy Spirit leads you.

Chapter 1: The Mystery of Emotions

1. Take time to get to know one another by sharing:

   - Your name
   - Your favorite thing to do
   - Why you joined this group
   - What you would like to get out of this study

2. How, in the past, have you viewed emotions? What are they and why do we have them?

3. Read Genesis 1:31. How does this apply to emotions?

4. Have you heard or believed that some emotions are bad? If so, which ones? Why?

5. Can the various forms of anger and fear ever be good?

6. Are emotions like jealousy or greed ever good?

7. What role did emotions play in Jesus' life?

8. Give an example of when your emotions helped you.

9. Give an example of when your emotions either led you astray or caused problems.

CHAPTER 2: THE SUBJECTIVE SIDE OF EMOTIONS

1. What did you especially like or dislike about this chapter? Why?

2. The chapter stated: "Because we have no way to 'get inside' of another person's head, we never really know exactly how another person is feeling or experiencing some event." Do you agree or disagree with this statement? Why?

3. Does the idea that we can never really know exactly how another person is feeling or experiencing some event have any importance to how you interact with others? Explain.

4. The chapter opened with the story of John's experience on the freeway and how it brought new meaning to things he learned about driving in school. Describe an incident when an experience aroused emotions that reinforced the importance of information you had learned.

5. How does your experience of a worship service differ when you are emotionally involved with it as opposed to when you are not emotionally involved?

6. The chapter stated, "Experiences that affect you in some important way receive an emotional 'stamp.' The emotions associated

with what you've learned then helps to order and regulate your behavior. They draw your attention and energy away from less important information and activities towards more important ones." How have your experiences as a Christian changed your understanding of God and what He wants?

7. Describe a time when you experienced a disappointment or loss and how God used it to make you more into the image of Christ and/or bless others.

8. Read John 15:1–4. What does Jesus mean when he speaks of being "fruitful"? (see Galatians 5:22–23; Romans 1:13; Colossians 1:3–7).

9. What does Jesus mean when he says "remain in me"? (see John 6:53–58 and verse 35; John 8:31–32; Luke 8:15). How do you do this?

10. Read Ephesians 4:14–16. What is the word picture that Paul is painting in these verses? What role does the church play in keeping you from being "tossed back and forth by the waves, and blown here and there by every wind of teaching"?

11. If you have been an active member of a church, what has it meant for you and your walk with God? How does your spiritual walk change when you become distant from your church?

CHAPTER 3: THE PHYSICAL SIDE OF EMOTIONS

1. What did you especially like or dislike about this chapter? Why?

2. Read Psalm 139:13–16. What new insights about how you are "fearfully and wonderfully made" did your gain from this chapter?

3. In describing how your brain does a lot of information processing that you are unaware of, this chapter used the example of driving a car. Describe a time when you were not paying attention while driving, but your mind alerted you to a turn you needed to make or to danger. How does this relate to your everyday life?

4. The chapter described how the amygdalae give an "emotional stamp" to memories associated with danger. Describe something that has happened to you, either positive or negative, that you will never forget.

5. How is this memory different from other memories that you have? How has this memory affected your life?

6. When has the fight or flight response described in the chapter helped you? When has it caused problems for you?

7. The chapter discussed the role that medications can play with emotional problems. Do you agree that medications can play a role in managing some emotional problems? Explain. If you disagree with this idea, describe why you disagree with it.

8. If you have found medications helpful when dealing with an emotional issue, describe your experience.

9. The Recommended Activities discussed the importance of spending time alone with God. Do you have a regular time alone with God? If not, what keeps you from doing this?

10. If you have a regular time for prayer and meditation, what do you do? How has this time alone with God changed your life?

11. What would you suggest to someone who wants to spend time alone with God but is finding it difficult?

CHAPTER 4: BEING A WISE STEWARD OF YOUR BODY

1. What did you especially like or dislike about this chapter? Why?

2. Read 1 Corinthians 6:19–20, Ephesians 2:21–22, Romans 12:1 and Romans 6:13. These verses describe how the body, as the temple of the Holy Spirit, is meant to be used to glorify God in service and worship and to become an instrument of righteousness. The application drawn from these verses is that we need to be wise stewards of the marvelous bodies we've been given. Do you agree? Why or why not?

3. What does "being a wise steward of your body" mean to you?

4. The chapter discussed the importance of getting sufficient sleep. Based on what you read, do you get enough sleep each day? Why or why not?

5. What has kept you from getting enough sleep in the past? How can you overcome this obstacle?

6. The chapter discussed the fourth commandment and "Sabbath rest." Do you take a Sabbath rest? If so, what do you do?

7. The chapter discussed the need to be aware of your "stress indicators" — signs that stress is interfering with your ability to think clearly and perform routine tasks. What key indicators did you identify?

8. Describe a time when you ignored signs that stress was starting to affect you adversely.

9. How could you reduce unnecessary activities during times of high stress? Be specific. Do you do this?

10. The chapter discusses the need to take more time with decisions and consult others when you are stressed. Describe a rash decision you made under stress that was not wise. How can you apply the idea of taking more time with decisions and consulting others to future occasions when you are stressed? Be specific.

11. How do you apply the idea of taking short breaks after times of intense activity? If you don't take short breaks, what could you do in the future? Be specific.

Chapter 5: THE MENTAL SIDE OF EMOTIONS

1. What did you especially like or dislike about this chapter? Why?

2. Read the story of David's encounter with King Saul described in 1 Samuel 24. How was David's interpretation of events different from that of his men? Why did David's men look at events so differently?

3. Describe a time when you interpreted an event very differently from someone close to you.

4. The chapter discussed how most of our emotions are the result of our interpretation of events. It diagrammed this process as:

Event ⟶ Interpretation ⟶ Emotion ⟶ Action

The chapter then discussed how interpretations that trigger emotions are tied in with your needs and can be divided into three broad categories:

• A need has been satisfied or may be satisfied
• A threat exists or may soon exist

• A loss of some sort has occurred or may occur

Describe an emotional reaction you experienced because of one of the above interpretations.

5. How has your walk with God and study of the Bible changed how you interpret events?

6. The chapter discussed how "knowing" something and "understanding" it are different. It further discussed how the difference is the result of experience as discussed in chapter 2. It also states that true understanding is reflected in changes in behavior. Describe a biblical truth that you have come to both know and understand as indicated by changes that have taken place in your behavior.

7. Describe a biblical truth that you know, but which your behavior indicates you still don't fully understand.

8. The chapter discusses how Satan is the "father of lies." What does this mean to you? How do you see this in the world around you?

9. The chapter listed several beliefs that underlie the commercials and programs you watch and the secular material you read. Describe two that you have observed.

10. Did any of these beliefs reflect how you sometimes think? If so, which ones? How?

CHAPTER 6: CORE BELIEFS

1. What did you especially like or dislike about this chapter? Why?

2. The chapter described how a fundamental change in a destructive core belief made a radical transformation in the

life of Claudia. Have you ever experienced a change like this? Explain.

3. The chapter explained that we are sometimes fully aware of our destructive core beliefs and that we also may not be fully aware of them. However, they are always reflected in how we think and act. As you looked at the examples of common destructive core beliefs, which did you identify as playing a role in your life in the past or present in each of the following areas:

- Yourself: your personality, strengths, and weaknesses
- The nature of relationships
- The world around you
- The nature of God

4. The chapter discussed how our core beliefs are usually a mixture of truth and destructive beliefs. What core beliefs that line up with biblical truth have helped you be what God wants you to be in each of the following areas:

- Yourself: your personality, strengths, and weaknesses
- The nature of relationships
- The world around you
- The nature of God

5. The chapter discusses the importance of periodic self-examination. Is this something you do? Why or why not?

6. If your answer was yes, share with the group when and how you practice self-examination.

7. Read 2 Corinthians 7:8–11. What is the difference between godly sorrow and worldly sorrow?

8. How can you resolve worldly sorrow?

9. The Recommended Activities presented the following model of how to approach someone you've wronged:

- Repent: "I'm sorry for what I did."
- Ask for forgiveness: "Please forgive me."
- Ask to make amends: "Is there anything I can do to make up for it?" (You may already know what you should do. If so, ask them, "May I . . . ")

Is this easy for you to do? Why or why not? What could help you do the above when it is appropriate?

CHAPTER 7: THE WINDOW OF THE SOUL

1. What did you especially like or dislike about this chapter? Why?

2. The chapter stated that there are many aspects of reality about which the Bible is either silent or very vague. What are areas of the Bible that you wish were more specific? Why?

3. How did you react to the idea that we need to become comfortable with not knowing? Is it easy or difficult for you to "not know" all the details? Explain.

4. What does "spiritual" mean to you?

5. How do you view the ideas of soul and spirit?

6. Read the following verses as shown in chapter 7: Psalm 43:5; Lamentations 3:20; Psalm 35:9; Hebrews 10:38 (NASB if available); Matthew 26:38; John 12:27; and Ephesians 6:6. Each of these verses uses the Hebrew or Greek word for "soul." How is this word being used in these verses?

7. Read the following verses as shown in chapter 7: Job 41:15–16; Zechariah 12:1; Ecclesiastes 12:7; John 3:8; Romans 8:16; and Luke 8:55. Each of these verses uses the Hebrew or Greek word for "spirit." How is this word being used in these verses?

8. What happens when we are separated from God?

9. The chapter stated that your emotions reveal your true spiritual condition. Do you agree or disagree? Explain.

10. Describe a time when your emotions revealed something to you about where you were spiritually that you didn't like.

11. Describe a time when your emotions revealed that true spiritual growth had occurred.

12. Share your experience when you did the recommended activity where you reflected on what your emotions reveal about your spiritual character.

CHAPTER 8: EMOTIONS AND GOD'S WILL FOR YOU

1. What did you especially like or dislike about this chapter? Why?

2. Read Proverbs 3:5–6, Psalm 32:8, and Ephesians 5:15–17. What are these verses saying?

3. This chapter stated: "The truth is that God's individual will for you is not a hidden secret that you have to seek out. God does not hide Himself or what He wants from you. In fact, the Bible is very clear that we are able to know God's will." Do you agree or disagree with this statement? Why?

4. What is God's moral will?

5. The chapter stated: "It turns out that what God wants is the same for every believer. It is not a specific rigid plan, but rather a goal: 'to be conformed to the likeness of his Son' (Romans 8:29)." It later states: "God's moral will *is* His individual will for you." Do you agree or disagree with this statement? Explain.

6. In the analogy of traveling from Sacramento to New York, the chapter stated that "God does sometimes give you a very personal and specific communication about a danger you are facing or something He wants you to do." Describe a time when God either had something that He wanted you to do or warned you about a danger.

7. The chapter stated that "one of the purposes of emotions is to share in the experience of love and joy that are the essence of God." How have you experienced this in your life?

8. The chapter stated: "In previous chapters, we've seen how emotions move us to take action and help us respond to danger, learn and prioritize information, and communicate with one another. Each of these functions of emotions has a spiritual side that, when functioning under the direction of the Holy Spirit, can alert us to spiritual dangers, enable us to understand God's nature and will, and help us listen and respond to God's leading." How have you experienced this aspect of emotions unfold as you have walked with God?

9. Read each of the commandments given in Exodus 20:1–17. Answer the following after you read each one (you may not have time to finish this question when done as a group; an alternative approach would be to break into groups of two or three and divide the commandments up; then re-form and report on what each group discussed):

- In your own words, what is this commandment saying?
- How does this apply to life in today's world?
- How does this apply to me?
- In what ways do I conform to this commandment?
- In what ways am I not conforming to it?

CHAPTER 9: HOW GOD SPEAKS TO YOU

1. What did you especially like or dislike about this chapter? Why?
2. Read Mark 7:21–22. How do these interfere with your relationship with God.

3. The chapter describes how unforgiveness can come in many forms such as bitterness, hatred, malice, holding grudges, and resentment. Describe a time when unforgiveness interfered with your relationship with God.

4. Read Matthew 6:24 and 1 John 2:15–17. Describe a time when you placed other things before God and how it affected your life.

5. Describe how your life is different when you are separated from Christ's body, the church, and when you are connected to it.

6. Which spiritual disciplines do you practice? Which are especially important to you?

7. How does your practice of the spiritual disciplines affect your faith and relationship with God?

8. What interferes with your practice of the disciplines? What helps you continue practicing spiritual disciplines?

9. Give an example of how God has:

- Used the Bible to speak to you

- Spoken to you through another person
- Spoken to you in some other way

10. Have you ever thought God was speaking to you when you were just fooling yourself because you wanted something very much? If so, share this experience and what you learned from it.

Chapter 10: Emotions that Come Out of the Blue

1. What did you especially like or dislike about this chapter? Why?

2. The chapter described the important role that conditioned emotional responses play in our daily life. One of these roles is the way we comfort ourselves, like Kim's fondness for Chinese almond cookies. What are some of the foods, places, or activities from childhood that you still use to comfort yourself? Describe how they developed when you were young and how you use them as an adult.

3. The chapter returned to the story of the blind men and elephant to describe how conditioned emotional responses become intertwined with core beliefs and spiritual issues. Take one conditioned emotional response you identified from the previous question and share how it is connected to one of your core beliefs and or a spiritual issue you are dealing with.

4. The chapter described a simple two-step approach for diminishing negative conditioned emotional responses called, "what's Happening, what's Real." Describe an experience you had while using this approach.

5. How did the people who raised you manage anger, fear, disappointment, sadness, and hurt?

6. Share one example of how the way in which you manage anger, fear, disappointment, sadness, or hurt was modeled after the people who raised you.

7. How have the ways that you manage your emotions that were modeled from your parents benefited or harmed you?

CHAPTER 11: EMOTIONS THAT ARE TABOO

1. What did you especially like or dislike about this chapter? Why?

2. Read Genesis 2:25. What changed the free and frank relationship Adam and Eve had with each other and God?

3. Why do people hide things from themselves, others, and God?

4. Describe an emotion that was uncomfortable for you in the past. Why do you think it was uncomfortable? What do you do when you feel this emotion today? Does it still make you uncomfortable? If not, what caused the change?

5. Read the example in the first exercise of the Recommended Activities for chapter 11. Is it easy or difficult for you to use accurate emotional language like this? If it is difficult, why do you think it is difficult?

6. When discussing the use of vague words to describe emotions, the Recommended Activities stated that it is sometimes appropriate to do this. Examples cited included social events where people simply are not interested in all the details of your life and times when you are dealing with people who are not trustworthy or safe. Is it easy or difficulty for you to be vague when you are in a situation where it is not appropriate or wise to share too much? Explain.

7. What type of emotional models did you have while growing up?

8. Were there any emotions that were either rarely or never shown in your home? Were any emotions labeled as being either wrong or bad in your home? Do these include emotions that you usually don't show or maybe never experience?

9. How has your way of managing emotions, learned during your formative years, influenced how you view God and interact with Him?

10. The chapter describes how becoming friendly with the emotions that have been taboo often allows you to address in an experiential way issues you have already identified mentally. Share how this has been true for you.

CHAPTER 12: TRUE EMOTIONAL HEALING

1. What did you especially like or dislike about this chapter? Why?

2. Read Ephesians 6:12. How have you experienced this truth in your life?

3. Read 1 Corinthians 2:14. The chapter discussed the example of Warren talking to a therapist who was working with a boy Warren was adopting. The therapist couldn't understand Warren's explanation of how he had made so much progress with the boy. Describe an experience you have had like this.

4. The chapter makes the statement, "All true healing comes from God through the Holy Spirit." It then gives the examples of J.W. and Cricket. How has this been true for your life?

5. The chapter describes the following six steps for managing emotions effectively.

Step 1: What Am I Feeling?
Step 2: What Triggered this Emotion?
Step 3: Was My Emotional Response Appropriate?
Step 4: Were the Actions I Took Appropriate?
Step 5: What Does God Want Me to Learn from This?
Step 6: Is There Some Action I Need to Take?

Describe a time when one or more of these steps were especially important for you.

6. Which of these steps is most difficult for you? Why?

7. Which step is most important for you?

8. What is the most important thing that you will take away from studying this book?

INDEX

ADDITIONAL BOOKS
BY RENEAU PEURIFOY

Anxiety, Phobias & Panic

Mr. Peurifoy's first work, now revised and in its third edition, was based on a program that was developed by the author over a period of eight years and which has become the standard for therapists and treatment centers around the world.

One of the unique features of this work is the way it is organized into a series of easy-to-follow lessons. This structured approach is the reason *Anxiety, Phobias & Panic* is used in treatment centers and self-help groups around the world. One of the most helpful aspects of *Anxiety, Phobias & Panic* is the list of recommended activities at the end of each lesson. The book is full of practical exercises showing the reader how to apply the concepts and ideas it presents. Instructions for the exercises are given step-by-step, in simple language.

Overcoming Anxiety

Overcoming Anxiety presents a unique approach to managing anxiety, offering readers a comprehensive and far-reaching philosophy that stresses lasting preventive measures over superficial—and often just temporary—antidotes. This groundbreaking book shows sufferers how to shift their focus from the messenger, or the symptoms of anxiety, to the message—the core cause of anxiety.

Like his first book, *Overcoming Anxiety* is structured as a series of lessons. However, the lessons are intertwined with three case histories drawn from the author's extensive clinical experience. By following these individuals through the process of recovery, you learn not only how to identify and challenge negative thinking patterns but also how to achieve control and change destructive and dysfunctional behavior. Each chapter ends with a set of recommended activities. Also included is an extensive resource guide.

Overcoming Anxiety can be used as a stand-alone program for learning how to personalize the valuable healing strategies set forth, paving the way for a more complete, lifelong recovery from the troubling afflictions of anxiety disorders. It is also a valuable follow-up for those who have read *Anxiety, Phobias & Panic* and would like additional skills.

ANGER: TAMING THE BEAST

Anger: Taming the Beast is unique among a host of books on anger because it is designed to be used both by people with explosive anger and those who suppress anger and tend to be non-assertive. The chapters take you step-by-step on the road to understanding why and how you get angry and teaches you how to express anger appropriately and effectively.

As you work through the book, you follow the case histories of four people who illustrate the principles and techniques being taught. The first two are a man and woman with explosive tempers. The second two are a man and a woman who find it difficult to express anger. By using these four individuals, Mr. Peurifoy is able to explore aspects of anger that are often omitted from other books on this subject.

Each chapter includes recommended activities at the end that help you apply the ideas presented.